LOST

IN TRANSITION

Lost In Transition
Becoming Spiritually Prepared For College

Ten Year Anniversary Edition

Tommy McGregor

To Webb, Wolf, Emily, Lauren, Danielle, & Melissa.

May you always know what it means
to live and love in Christ!

CONTENTS

INTRODUCTION

SECTION 1: TRANSITION

SECTION 2: TRANSFORM

SECTION 3: TRANSCEND

SECTION 4: ADDITIONAL RESOURCES

END NOTES

INTRODUCTION
BEGINNING THE JOURNEY

College ...some of the best years of your life ... guaranteed or your money back. Well, probably not, but your years in college will mean much more than just the degree you receive on graduation day. College is a rite of passage that you experience and never forget. It is the time when you cross over from kid to adult. It represents a pre-"real world" period that will prepare you for the rest of your life. While in college, it is very likely that you will meet some of your closest friends, decide on a career path, make many lasting memories, and according to statistics, have a great chance of meeting your future spouse.

For most of you, college is the first time in your life that you are truly out on your own. It's one step into adulthood ...yet one foot is still evenly planted in the world of sleeping in, staying out late, and napping in the middle of the afternoon. College is the place where you will learn what life is all about—not just academically, but socially, relationally, and hopefully spiritually. During those amazing four years (or five or six …), you will basically grow up. When you were a kid, you were taught the fundamentals of life. As a child you learned how to walk, then how to run, and then how to ride a bike. In middle school, you learned about human behavior after noticing for the first time that the girl/guy sitting next to you in math class looked cute. In high school, it was all about relationships. You had best friends, first dates, former best friends, more dates, break ups, new former best friends, and so on as you began to develop all that you have learned over the years to create who you are today.

And now it's time for college. Sure, you signed up for college because it was the logical next step. Maybe you had always planned to go, or possibly you are being forced to try it. Either way, you are taking life to the next level, and you have the opportunity to learn and grow into the person you have always wanted to be. I remember back in my high school days, dreaming about how it was going to be in college. I think I got senioritis around the ninth grade and college fever by the eleventh grade. I spent many days in senior economics class thinking about being away at school and on my own. My guess is you've shared that daydream. I will tell you this: the college experience you dreamed about in high school will not exactly be the college experience you will walk away with on the day you graduate. Hopefully it will be better. It could be worse. Why? Because college will not be like anything you have ever experienced before. You are truly blazing a new trail now.

To succeed at this level of life, you have to put to use all that you have learned up to this point. Anytime you make a transition from one stage of life to another, you have to be prepared. Transitions can be difficult to navigate, and most high school graduates face the move to college as their first major life change. I have heard people compare the high school-to-college transition with the shift from middle school to high school. I think the high school-to-college transition is more like your first day of the first grade. Remember that day? I do! I remember my parents leaving me in an unfamiliar place with people I didn't know, and I cried and cried and cried ... No wait, that was my first day at college! The transition may be hard, but once you make it, the experience can be incredible.

BALANCING IN A NEW CURRENT

I promise not to bore you with lots of mindless statistics that may or may not mean anything to you in the first place (they say that 84.3 percent[1] of all statistics are wrong anyway). But I would like to share with you one statistical range that I believe is very important to understand as you prepare to transition from high school to college.

Depending on which statistic you look at, around three-fourths[2] of all Christian high school seniors drift away from growth in their relationship with Jesus within twelve months of graduation. That means, statistically, between you and the two who sit on either side of you in your second period class in high school, only one of you will continue to pursue a growing relationship with Jesus during your freshman year in college. Now, before you begin to think about who in your senior class will certainly be the one to struggle, just remember, it could be you. Don't think so? Neither did I.

So, why is this statistic so real? Here is where this problem originates. Think for a moment about the influences that you have had in your life during high school. For most Christian high school seniors, there have been four major influences in their lives: family, friends, church, and mentors. If you come from a family that models a life in Christ, then you are very fortunate and blessed. Hopefully, you have had a church that has taught you how to walk in Christ, as well as a mentor that has discipled you and helped you to grow in your relationship with Jesus. Most likely, you have also had Christian friends to lean on as you have grown up together. These four influences have helped to construct a spiritual infrastructure for your life during your years in high school. The problem is that few if any of these influences will be with you in college. You may have some of your high school friends in college with you, but for the most part, the support will not be there. You might be going to school in your hometown, living at home, and continuing to attend the same church, but it will still be different.

By the time you are a senior in high school, you are flowing in a current. You know where to go for discipleship, accountability, and fellowship. Unless you recently moved to a new school or church or had a major family change, you are flowing in a comfortable current by your senior year in high school. So, the logical assumption for many is that if they can continue to stay steady as they move on to college, then they will be fine. They remember how they did it in high school, and so they try to continue to do it the same way in college. What they don't factor in is that the current in college is different than in high school. It's not that you can't do it; it is that you have to understand how to do it differently. You must learn how to balance in the new current.

I don't need to tell you that college can be an extremely spiritually distracting environment where only the strong survive. But, I would like you to understand that the first step to survival is in the transition. The word transition simply means the process of change. Just like going from junior high to high school, college to career, or single life to marriage, when you are moving to another phase of your life, you must prepare yourself for that change.

YOUR TRANSITION YEAR

If you are reading this sometime in the year of your high school graduation, you are in what I call your Transition Year. Your Transition Year begins in January of your last semester of high school and ends in December, after your first semester of college. During this twelve-month period, your life will be in major transition. This is a really fun time of life with lots of potential for growth and maturity. Inevitably that also means that this could be a year of major confusion of your identity and direction in life.

I am convinced that the secret to making college a truly great experience is the same thing that makes life a truly great experience. As special as those years in college may be, one thing in life is clearly most important: a healthy, growing relationship with Jesus Christ. Just think, the God of the universe wants to know you intimately and personally. I'm not talking about a religion of do's and don'ts, rights and wrongs, rituals and rules, but rather a relationship with Jesus that is an ongoing, day-by-day experience that does not end after four years and a final exam. God created you for a personal relationship, and He desires to know you and wants to be the central focus of your life.

This book is for those who desire that relationship. This book is for recent, or soon-to-be, high school graduates heading to college, or college freshman beginning their college experience. For some, this book will be read over and over and consumed as the reader walks and grows in Christ. For others, it needs to be put in a drawer, or on a shelf with an invisible "break glass in emergency" sign on it. I do recommend that you try to read this book during your Transition Year, but above all, this book needs to be read when the time is right.

This book is divided into three sections: Transition, Transform, and Transcend. These are what I call the three steps of change. Transition is the process of change from one stage of life to another. You may have already gone through some life transitions, but for many graduating seniors, this is often the first. The second stage is transform, which means to begin to adapt to this new phase by taking control of the change rather than letting it take control of you. The third step is transcend, which is learning to excel in this new stage of life. In order to make a healthy transition to college, focus will need to be placed on each of these three steps.

There are questions at the end of each chapter. I hope that you will view these questions as a part of the chapter and answer them as you read. I highly recommend that you read this book with other people for purposes of discussion and accountability. If you are reading this book as part of a small group, take a chapter at a time and go over the questions together. If you are reading it individually, find a friend to read it with and set up a time to discuss your thoughts. I suggest that you get a notebook or journal to keep your thoughts and answers to the questions. This is the second edition of this book, and for the past few years, I have heard from readers of the original version that most would read the book with a small group in the spring and then go back and reread their notes, underlines, and answers during the fall semester of college.

This book serves as a guide to help you make a healthy transition into college. In the back section you will find a study guide and other transition materials like a monthly checklist and more. Also, I hope that you will go to the website www.thetransmission.org and find more content in the form of articles, devotionals, videos, and more to help you with the transition to college. I believe that the more you dive into preparing for this transition, the smoother and more healthy that transition will be.

BEGIN WITH THE END IN MIND

Before we begin I would like to ask you this key question that I hope will challenge you to be serious about the spiritual transition to college: Are you as spiritually mature right now as you want to be on the day you graduate from college? In other words, at the age of seventeen or eighteen, are you willing to cease growth in your walk with Christ and find yourself at the age of twenty-two or twenty-three with the faith maturity of a teenager? I certainly hope not.

Life is a journey. It is made to be enjoyed, embraced, and experienced. In John 10:10, Jesus says, "I have come that you might have life to the fullest."[3] Are you willing to live a life of purpose, a life full of opportunity and adventure? God created this life journey and wants you to join Him there. Come on!

TRANSITION
SECTION ONE

Chapter One
BOUND TO CHANGE

Ashley just got home from her high school graduation practice. At the practice, Ashley's class did a formal walkthrough in the auditorium and found out where their seats would be for the big event tomorrow night. Ashley was excited about graduation and can hardly wait to become a college student. That night before going to sleep, Ashley lay in bed, thinking about her years in high school. She thought about how it just seemed like yesterday that she was a nervous high school freshmen and now that was all over. She thought about all the friends and memories she made in high school and about how she will be starting over in just a few months as a college freshman.

"What is college going to be like?" Ashley asked herself in the quiet of her bedroom. "What if I don't make friends fast? What if I don't get into a good sorority? What if I don't get along with my roommate?" As Ashley thought back to high school and looked forward to college, she thought about the most important question yet: "What if I don't find a group of friends who are Christians and want to grow in their faith?" She had heard recently that most Christian students fall away from their faith

within a year of their high school graduation. She was quick to think that she wouldn't do that but deep down knew she could.

Ashley knew she had a choice to make. She wasn't sure what that choice was or how to begin to make it, but she knew deep down that she needed to be responsible for her faith and do whatever she could to spiritually protect herself. She turned off the light, tucked herself in bed, and started to pray about her life at college, knowing that very soon her life was bound to change.

On the night of your high school graduation, life changes; a page is turned. Once you move the tassel from the right to the left, you grow a little further away from being a kid and a lot closer to becoming an adult. You have worked hard to get where you are, and you have a lot of fun memories to show for it. My guess is your spiritual life has been up and down, strong and weak. For most people your age, that is the case. If you took your faith seriously in high school, you may have been stronger than others, but being a teenager is hard, and trying to grow in your faith during those years is even harder. Most Christian high school students I know are still learning how to balance the pressures of high school with the faithfulness of following Jesus. But now high school is coming to an end (if not already over), and you can't go back.

Now it's time to go to the next level of life—college. Regardless of whether you are going to a big school or a small one, a school in your hometown or one halfway across the country, there is no doubt that things are about to change. I was five years old when my oldest sister graduated from high school and went off to college. I vaguely remember the day we moved her into the freshman dorm at the University of Alabama. According to my parents, I understood that she was going away to live at college, but between having to balance the demands of the kindergarten social scene and daily episodes of Captain Kangaroo,[4] it just did not fully compute. After spending the day unloading her stuff, we said good-bye and started the two-hour trip home. About a block away from campus, reality began to sink in, and I realized that my sister was not coming home with us. At the next red light, I jumped out of the car with eyes full of tears and ran through the traffic back to her dorm.

Going off to college means things will change. You too will pack your things and move away from the life you have always known. College means you will have to make yourself go to class, study for tests, wake up for that 8:00 a.m. chem lab, and of course, continue to grow in your relationship with God. College is a big step, and you must be prepared (and you just might have to prepare your younger brother/sister, too).

THOSE WERE THE DAYS

Starting college is the end of a chapter in your life and the beginning of a new one. Once you graduate from high school, those days are over and gone. Never again will you have those experiences, with those friends, in the same places. I understand that for some of you this is a relief and for others the thought of leaving the life that you've known is a sad one. It might be months or even years after high school that you think on those days fondly. My friend Daniel just graduated from high school, and he was so ready. He had moved on in his mind and heart way before graduation day came and actually had a countdown on Facebook for months counting down to the big day. Another friend, Lauren, cried for days after she walked out of her school for the final time because she had connected so much to life as a high school senior and, though she was excited about college, had to mourn the end of an era. I think both are okay! Recently I was riding in the car with my friend Lunden and his parents. Lunden was one year out of Baylor University when we passed by his old high school that he had graduated from five years before, and he had a moment. As I was looking at the football field and thinking about it full of people, my friend said to his parents and me, "Man, I had some great times in that place!" It was like he was just flipping back a couple of chapters in his life for the first time and remembering the good times in high school with his friends. It may take a few months or years, or it might only take a few steps out of the building, but hopefully at some point, you will cherish fond memories from high school as you move on with your life.

BECOMING YOU 2.0

Before moving off to college, everyone has to pack. You go through your closets, drawers, and shelves and decide what to take and what to leave. Since your life is in a big transition phase anyway, you can use this one to your advantage. As you begin to cram all of your stuff into a suitcase, you can also pack all of your dreams, ambitions, and hopes into a bag and choose to leave many of your struggles, obstacles, and fears behind. Let me ask you this question: If you could change a few things about yourself, what would they be? I don't mean being taller or having curly hair, I mean things about your character or your habits. On the next page, make a list of a few things that you would like to change about yourself. This is a list of things that, if you could go back in time and start over, you would do differently. Let me get you started. If you had asked me that question when I was your age, I probably would have said: (1) Find a couple of close friends to really be open with and share deep stuff with, rather than always being on the surface with everyone. (2) Spend more time thinking about God and praying. (3) Get more involved in school leadership opportunities like SGA, etc. Below, make your own list.

1.

2.

3.

4.

When you go to college, you can become anyone you want to be. This can be a very healthy thing for you, or it can become dangerous. Going off to college can be a time of new spiritual beginnings. Paul says to those who put their faith in Christ, "They are not the same anymore, for the old life is gone. A new life has begun."[5] Probably the best thing about life transitions is that you have an opportunity to make changes in your life. As you move off to college, you are going to a new place with new people. Even if you have friends from high school going to the same school as you are, you can still make changes in who you are and how you act. As you transition into college, you can become the person you've just listed above. This is your time to develop as a person and as a follower of Christ. Do you want to have a better GPA than you had in high school? Here is your chance. Would you like to have more friends and feel like you belong in your social group? This is your opportunity. Want to live a life of purpose? Then let your college transition be a spiritual transition. When a company puts out a new version of an older product, it is often called the 2.0 version. It is better than the previous one because it has been more developed. You will change as you grow in college, and if you grow in the direction of improving yourself, then you have the opportunity to develop into "You 2.0."

THE FIRST STEP

The first step to making a successful spiritual transition into college begins with a commitment to following Christ. Let me begin by asking you this question: Do you have a personal relationship with Jesus Christ? Have you ever honestly asked Him to forgive you of your sins and come into your life? Since you are a student, let's take a test. Can you answer "yes" to all of the following three questions without a hint of doubt? If not, then we need to make sure you understand what a relationship with God really is. So, if you would get out your number 2 pencil and sit quietly until I say you can begin ... Go!

1. Have I given my life over to Jesus Christ and know that if I died right now, I would go to heaven?

(circle one) Yes No Maybe

2. Do I actively seek God in a growing relationship through the way I think and the things I do?

(circle one) Yes No Maybe

3. Do my friends at school and those I spend time with on weekends know me as a Christian and think of me as someone who stands up for what I believe?

(circle one) Yes No Maybe

So, how did you do on the test? Were you totally honest with yourself? If you answered "no" or "maybe" to even one of those questions, then join me as we look deeper into what an active relationship with God is. I mean it can't hurt, right? For those of you who circled "yes" to all three questions, I feel like the rest of this chapter will be a healthy review for you.

Being a Christian and walking with God is about a relationship. As I said before, it is not about rules and rituals; it is about knowing your Creator and actively growing in a relationship with Him. I love basketball, and in my opinion, Michael Jordan is the greatest basketball player ever. Here's a guy who is a five-time NBA MVP, won six world championships, and still holds more records than any other player in history.[6] I used to love to watch him play and even had the opportunity to see him play in person a few times, but I do not know Michael Jordan. As a matter of fact, we've never even met. Even though I know a lot about Jordan and admire him, I could never say that we have a relationship.

There is a big difference between knowing God and knowing about God. You can go to church, hear the stories, even read the Bible and find out lots of great things about God, but it's not until you put your faith in Him, letting Him come into your life and make it real, that you begin the journey. In order to do this, you must understand a few things:

1. **Jesus is the Son of God and is God in the flesh.** Colossians 1:15 says, "He is the visible image of the invisible God, the firstborn over all creation," and John 1:14 tells us that "The Word became flesh and made his dwelling among us. We have seen his glory, the glory of the One and Only, who came from the Father, full of grace and truth."

2. **There is an enemy of God, and he desperately wants to keep you from becoming the person that you were created to be.** In John 10:10 Jesus tells us that we have two options for life. One is life in Him that is abundant and full. The other is one in which we allow Satan, called the thief in this verse, to come in and "kill, steal, and destroy." First Peter 5:8 describes him as a "roaring lion looking for someone to devour."

3. **Jesus died for you and can save you from your sins and from spiritual death.** Romans 3:23 says, "For all have sinned and fall short of the glory of God," and Romans 6:23 says, "For the wages of sin is death, but the gift of God is eternal life in Christ Jesus our Lord." John 3:16 says, "For God so loved the world that he gave his one and only Son, that whoever believes in him shall not perish but have eternal life," and in John 14:6, "Jesus answered, 'I am the way and the truth and the life. No one comes to the Father except through me.'"

4. **Jesus is waiting for you to ask Him into your life and begin the journey.** In Revelations 3:20, Jesus says, "Here I am! I stand at the door and knock. If anyone hears my voice and opens the door, I will come in and eat with him, and he with me." First Timothy 2:3-4 says, "This is good, and

pleases God our Savior, who wants all men to be saved and to come to a knowledge of the truth."

The choice to make Christ real in your life is really as easy as A, B, C.

Admit that you are a sinner. As I've already stated, the Bible says, "For all have sinned and fallen short of the glory of God"[7] and "The wages of sin is death."[8] In order for Jesus to forgive you, you must first admit your sin. This doesn't mean that you have to understand how to overcome your sinful ways. It just means that you must acknowledge that you have sinful ways because you can't possibly overcome your sin on your own.

Believe that Jesus is the Son of God and that He died on the cross to save you from your sins. Since the payment due for sin is death, Jesus chose to die for you so you would not have to. The second part of Romans 6:23 is, "but the gift of God is eternal life." Just like a gift that you might receive on your birthday, there is nothing you did to earn it, and there is nothing you can do to lose it. You don't deserve this gift, but rather it is offered to you out of grace. You must learn to believe in this gift because it is the central principle in the Christian faith.

Commit to following Jesus on the journey. This is the main ingredient to your walk with Christ. Without the commitment, you have gotten to the trailhead of the journey, with your pack on your back, but have refused to start walking. Many people admit and believe but never commit. Churches are full of "A-B people." These are individuals who go to church and live a moral life but never commit to the relationship with Jesus. According to the Bible, even the demons believe that Jesus is the Son of God. As author John Stott says, "Becoming a Christian is one thing; being a Christian is another."[9] The commitment in Jesus comes in following His lead. If you look in the Gospels, Jesus asked people to follow Him. This is the same question He poses to us today.

This decision to follow Jesus right now could not be a more important one. As we have already addressed, college can be a very spiritually distracting place. Satan, the enemy, stays pretty busy on college campuses. Why? Because he knows that college is filled with young people who are all experiencing many freedoms for the first time and are very vulnerable physically, relationally, socially, emotionally, and spiritually. I hope that you will understand that a full life in Christ will be better than a stolen, broken life without Him.

In 1836, Texas was fighting for its independence from Mexico. On February 23 the

Texas army of less than two hundred men was led by Colonel William B. Travis and found themselves surrounded by Mexican forces at the Alamo. The night before the Mexican army would attack, General Santa Anna sent a message that offered to spare the life of any man who chose to flee before sunrise. After announcing this option to his men, General Travis drew a line in the dirt and stated that if any man wished to stay and fight, he must step over that line. All but one man stepped over the line and fought to his death. Those men recognized an opportunity to stand up for a cause greater than themselves. Because of that battle at the Alamo, Santa Anna's army was depleted, and it was not long before Sam Houston defeated the Mexican army, which led Texas to victory and independence.[10]

Jesus has drawn a line in the sand. He has died for you and is asking you to follow Him. Jesus says in Luke 9:23, "If anyone would come after me, he must deny himself and take up his cross daily and follow me." He wants a relationship with you and desires for you to live the life you were created for. But first you must cross that line.

If you are ready to cross the line and give your life over to God, stop right now and pray about it. Tell God how you feel. If you are afraid or doubtful, tell Him that. If you are concerned about what your friends might say, tell Him and ask Him to help you through it. Once you admit and believe,

He will forgive you, come into your life, and never leave. Then it is up to you to spend the rest of your life practicing the commitment part of the deal. Once you pray to begin a relationship with God, find someone to talk to about it. This could be a parent, teacher, friend, or a mentoring figure. It is important that you let others know of your decision to follow Jesus so that they can help you in your journey.

If you are not ready to pray that prayer, you might want to put this book down and wait until you are. Remember I told you in the introduction that some of you will wait until you hit rock bottom before you get serious about your faith. If you choose not to continue on the journey, I suggest that you never stop asking questions. Don't be afraid to search for the truth. God will wait for you. But remember, by not accepting Jesus Christ, you are making a choice not to choose the abundant life offered in John 10:10.

When I was in college, I had a friend named Tim. Tim was the younger brother of one of my fraternity pledge brothers, and so when he came to college we were all excited to get to know him. Tim did not grow up in a Christian environment and was not a follower of Christ. It wasn't that he was knowingly rejecting Jesus; he was really unaware that he needed God in his life. It was obvious to me, though. Tim had a natural sense of compassion for others, and I felt that if he would ever began to follow Christ, then those gifts, and many others, would change lives. Fast-forward a decade or so, I had lost contact with Tim until I found him on Facebook. He had married the girl that he began to date after I graduated. She was a Christian. I saw online that he was not only a believer but a Sunday school teacher and a great dad and husband. I am so grateful that Tim finally gave his life to his Creator. He regrets missing all the years that he didn't know Jesus but seems to be making up for lost time now.

HITTING THE TRAIL

One summer years ago, I took a group of high school students to Colorado for an adventure at a place called Wilderness Ranch.[11] Wilderness Ranch is a backpacking camp located in the Rocky Mountains. We arrived at Wilderness in time for training, packing, and the last supper (or at least the last good one for a week). Early the next morning, our group left on a six-day, forty-mile hike. A bus took us to the trailhead and dropped us off. My group consisted of six of my high school friends, another Young Life leader, myself, and two trail guides who began as friends and, by the end, seemed to us like real-life super heroes. We started out on the trail, and for the first hour, I was thinking that this was going to be easy. By the end of the first day I thought, I can do this! But by the third day, I was on my knees telling God if He would just get me through this week, I'd promise to pray more, be nicer to people, and give all my possessions to the poor.

That trip was the most physically challenging event of my life. The trail went up the mountain, down the mountain, over the hills, and through the woods. At one point we even had to attach ourselves to a rope that was strung thirty feet above roaring whitewater and pull ourselves thirty feet across in order to pick up the trail on the other side. Two days into the trip, I got a bad case of altitude sickness that left me twelve thousand feet up, in the woods, with flu-like symptoms. It was bad. Yet at the same time, it was one of the greatest camping trips that I have ever had.

First, we saw some amazing sights. I can still remember the feeling after we all climbed a "fourteener" and the look on the faces of my high school friends when we saw the view. Second, we laughed together. My friend Andy had refused to relieve himself (in the solid form) during the entire trip. We were instructed to excuse ourselves from the group when nature called, take the community shovel, dig a hole, and do the deal. Andy did not feel like he could do that. For days he complained about stomach cramps but still stood for his boycott. Since we were so high up in the mountains, we had not seen anyone else for days.

We were isolated. Suddenly (and I mean pretty suddenly) Andy felt the urge to abandon his commitment, so he asked for the shovel and ran to a tree further down the trail. Then, while he was taking care of business, in an area of much lower altitude than we had been, a family on horseback passed by Andy's chosen location during the middle of the process. It was embarrassing for Andy and the family, but hilarious to the rest of us.

We saw amazing sights, laughed together, and we also experienced God together. One of my friends, Caleb, had been struggling. He had resisted a relationship with God for all of the two years that I knew him, yet on the last night in the quiet of the mountainous forest, Caleb realized that the goal of life was to commit to Christ and walk in a relationship with him. He and I prayed to God that night, and his life changed.

Your spiritual journey is similar to my week hiking in the Rockies. The day you start down the trail, you will be excited and ready for the ride of your life; your bags are packed and your Guide is there to walk with you the whole way. You will experience some great sights, share some great life moments with friends, and encounter God in the midst of your adventure. This journey will be abundant (John 10:10) and sufficient (2 Corinthians 12:9). Jesus promises not only to be there with you but to carry you when the road gets steep (Matthew 11:28). I'm not going to tell you that walking with

Jesus is easy. The Bible is full of stories and examples of followers of Christ who suffered because of it, but if we had the chance to ask, I'll bet these guys would say they wouldn't have traded anything for it.

FOLLOW THE LEADER

Just like hiking for a week in the Rockies, the key to your life's journey is to follow the Leader. Before Jesus officially began His ministry, He went to some local fishermen. These men did not wake up that morning knowing that they were about to go on the ultimate journey of a lifetime. They had no idea that the path they were about to take was going to eventually lead them to death. But when Jesus told them to follow, they went. In Luke 5, Jesus was preaching from the shore of the Sea of Galilee. It was there that he met Simon Peter, a local fisherman who was not having a very productive day at the office. Jesus told Peter to go out deeper and fish from the other side of the boat, but Peter explained that he had been out there all night long and had caught nothing. However, out of respect for Jesus, he went back out. Then in verses 6-11 we read,

> *This time their nets were so full they began to tear! A shout for help brought their partners in the other boat, and soon both*

boats were filled with fish and on the verge of sinking. When Simon Peter realized what had happened, he fell to his knees before Jesus and said, "Oh, Lord, please leave me —I'm too much of a sinner to be around you." For he was awestruck by the size of their catch, as were the others with him. His partners, James and John, the sons of Zebedee, were also amazed. Jesus replied to Simon, "Don't be afraid! From now on you'll be fishing for people!" And as soon as they landed, they left everything and followed Jesus.[12]

These guys left their families and the place they called home to follow Jesus. They blindly walked into unknown territory, unsure and insecure about their purpose and their future. Sound familiar?

Chapter Two
WHO DO YOU THINK THAT YOU ARE?

Andrew grew up in a Christian home and was active at his church and in other Christian organizations at his school. His parents taught him about living for Christ from the time he was in elementary school. He had a group of Christian friends that he spent most of his time with in high school and even served in Christian leadership positions in his school and church. From the time Andrew was in the seventh grade, he was involved in a weekly Bible study, learning about Jesus and how to grow in his faith.

When Andrew graduated from high school, he was excited to go to a big state university that was rich in athletic tradition and couldn't wait to experience it all. Even though Andrew knew that his new school was notorious for being a "party school," he was surprised to see what college life was all about when he arrived on campus. In the first couple of days of his first semester, Andrew found that the pressures of living outside the Christian bubble he had grown up in were difficult to manage. Within a few months, Andrew found himself involved in habits that he would not have had in high school. Andrew started drinking, and before the end of his first semester, he began doing drugs. At first, he did not think about the contrast of his life over the past year, but his childhood friend and roommate noticed the drastic changes in Andrew's life and called him out on his behavior. After realizing how far he had drifted, Andrew stopped and looked at his life. What had changed? It wasn't just that he had started smoking and drinking, but his language, outlook on life, and the way he treated others also had negatively changed. It had also dawned on him that he had never gone this long without thinking about God.

Andrew had to do some soul searching. He began asking himself questions like "How did this happen? Who am I?" Within one semester of college, Andrew was having an identity crisis and wasn't sure what to do next.

Once upon a time … That is usually how a good story begins, and we all love a good story. The plot is created, and we find ourselves engrossed in the characters of the tale: Lucy, Edmund, Peter, and Susan find themselves in the land of Narnia;[13] Frodo inherits the Ring and learns of its power;[14] Harry discovers that he is a wizard and is invited to Hogwarts School;[15] Buzz and the other toys are accidentally sent to Sunnyside Day Care, and it's up to Woody to help them escape.[16] A good story is usually filled with adventure, love, conflict, resolution, and a happy ending. These are the elements of a great story because they are the elements of God's story.

God's story is the account of our reality. It is the story that all others are founded on, and it is the basis of your story. Did you know that you had a story? You do, but to understand it, we first must look at God's story. Unlike all others, God's story didn't begin with "Once upon a time" but rather with "In the beginning." This is why God's story is so special; it is the original story. The setting opens as God created the world that we all know. Within this creation, God made man. Man was the greatest of all of God's creation because man was created in God's image. Soon after God created mankind, as you know, they fell into temptation and sinned against God. Later in the story, God orchestrated a rescue mission to win us back. He sent Jesus, His only Son, into the world to take our sin and redeem our relationship with God. God's story is one of unconditional love and is the story of all people, even those who don't yet see it.

When I was a high school senior, I wanted to do something memorable, something special that I could be remembered for. One morning that fall, I was reading the announcements over the school-wide intercom as part of my first period office aid job, and I discovered my opportunity. I was asked to read the rules for the homecoming queen election. These guidelines stated that to be eligible to run for homecoming queen, you had to be a senior, have at least a C average, and you had to have gone to the school for the entire semester.

(Apparently, they were afraid that a student would be HC queen at one school and then controversially transfer to another school and get it again.) It also said that to run, you would have to get 100 signatures, within the next five days, of people who would consider voting for you (to weed out those who didn't have a chance, I guess).

After reading this to the student body, I quickly realized that it never said that you had to be a female to run for our school's homecoming queen. It was in that moment that I declared my candidacy for homecoming queen of my high school. Even though I was given five days to get 100 signatures, I got over 300 between second and third period. By lunch I had a campaign manager, and before the end of the day, I had a creative director who was going to draw up a design for posters and T-shirts. Before school was over on that Monday, I proudly turned in my form, four days early, proving that a good homecoming "queen" was also punctual.

The next morning, the principle asked to have a word with me. I didn't know what he wanted to talk about, at first, until I saw my signature sheet on his desk. Needless to say, he didn't look very happy with me. He shut his door, which was never a good sign, and just stared at me for a moment almost wondering how to begin. After an ultra-awkward amount of silence, he simply asked, "Who do you think you are?" Not sure if the question was rhetorical or not, I began to answer, but he didn't want to hear it (which confirmed to me that it was truly rhetorical). He explained to me that he couldn't allow me to run for homecoming queen. I pleaded with him, attempting to paint a picture of the half-time ceremony: there I would be, center field ...with my mom! But he told me that he would not let me run for two reasons: one, because he said that he was afraid that I would win (can anyone say moral victory?) and, two, because, as he put it, that wasn't who I was.

I left the principal's office that morning with my head hung low, knowing that my dreams and aspirations of becoming the homecoming queen were spoiled (a reality that I got over before the end of the school day). The more I thought about it, the more I knew that my principal was right. That wasn't who I was. As a matter of fact, it would have been pretty stupid. Was that really how I wanted to be remembered? And also, was I willing to rob a deserving friend of such an honor as homecoming queen just because I wanted to get a laugh? So often we lose sight of who we are, and we try to be something else. Whatever the reason might be, we forfeit our pursuit of who we really are to become something that we truly don't want to be. When we do this, we move further away from who God made us to be and closer to someone that we don't recognize.

WHAT DO YOU WANT TO BE WHEN YOU GROW UP?

I think that every kid has been asked that question at least once: "What do you want to be when you grow up?" For me, I started out wanting to be a garbage man because they got to ride on the back of a huge truck. Then someone reminded me that firemen got to do that as well, plus they got to put out fires. That's when I knew I had to be a fireman when I grew up. Not long after, I changed it to be a doctor and then a rock star (that one I don't think I've totally outgrown yet). For every kid the answer is different, but still the question remains, "What do you want to be when you grow up?"

Chances are you are still getting that age-old question, but now it might be phrased in a more suitable way like "What do you want to major in when you get to college?" But my question to you is a much deeper question that I hope you will answer for yourself even before finding a major. My question isn't "What do you want to be?" but rather "Who do you want to be?" The reason I asked that is because self-discovery is a difficult task when you are in the middle of a life transition. It's better to have an idea of who you are before you go to college than to become someone you're not once you get there.

Do you know the story in the Bible about Jesus and the rich young man? It's in Luke 18.

Here was a wealthy young guy who asked Jesus what it took to gain eternal life. Jesus said that he should obey the commandments, and the young man said that he did. Then Jesus looked into his heart and said that he should give all of his money to the poor and follow Him. This made the man very sad because he had too much money to give it up, and he left. This is the only story in the Bible, that I can think of, that someone came searching for God, found out what it would take, and left empty handed. This man's answer to my question would have been, "I want to be rich!" This was who he thought he was, and it owned him. Jesus, on the other hand, knew this man better than he knew himself, and Jesus knew that this young man could be so much more if he would follow Jesus. Just speculating for a minute, let's say that this man had chosen to give his money to the poor and follow Jesus. Chances are we would have been reading more about him later in the New Testament. He might have funded the spread of the gospel all over the world. That would have changed the course of the world. Then, through the grace of God, he might have been able to go back to the source of his wealth and make more money in which he might have given even more to the poor. Today this man might have been known in history as Bob the Generous or something other than just the Rich Young Ruler. Amazing things will happen in our life when we choose to take a risk in the name of

Jesus. Unfortunately, this man never got to find that out.

Before you get to college, you must decide who you are going to be. Will you be the person that others want you to be, or will you be the person that God wants you to be? Just like with the young rich man, Jesus might be asking you to give up something that is standing in the way of a relationship with Him. When this happens, we must realize that a life in Christ far outweighs anything else that we can achieve on our own. Remember, it was the man with great wealth that was searching for real life. There will be nothing, now or in college, that will fill your life like an active, growing relationship with Jesus: not your friends, a boyfriend/girlfriend, grades, achievements, honors, experiences, or feelings. Jesus is asking us to follow Him, and that's who we want to be!

AVOIDING IDENTITY THEFT

Each year hundreds of thousands of Americans become victims to a crime called identity theft. This often starts when someone steals a credit card or a personal form of identification, like a social security number, and poses as that person. Then, usually after it is too late, the victimized person finds themselves lost, with their name and credit ruined. It takes years to recover from identity theft. Some victims never truly recover.

As bad as it would be for this to happen to you, there is another type of identity theft that is potentially more dangerous and life destroying. Personal and financial identity theft is damaging on so many levels, but spiritual identity theft could be even more devastating. It's one thing for a thief to steal your name. It's another thing for you to lose sight of who you are in the eyes of God and go on living your life outside of the plan and purpose that you were created for.

So, how does this happen? Well, it can take shape in so many ways, but the source of them all is a three-step internal scam: distract, disconnect, and deceive. Remember in chapter one, I mentioned the thief of John 10:10 that comes to "kill, steal, and destroy." This is Satan, and he is for real. When a thief steals your identity, he distracts you somehow and then disconnects you from that identity. In spiritual identity thief, Satan distracts you from your pursuit of following Christ with something that he knows is attractive to you. This might be a sinful struggle or possibly a path with greener grass. Once you begin to veer off course, you become more and more disconnected from your relationship with Jesus. Eventually, you become deceived by thinking that you are somehow better off this way, and without even knowing it, your identity in Christ has been stolen.

I have never seen this happen more prevalently than during the transition from high school to college. It often begins during your senior year. You are tired of the routine of old, knowing that freedom is just around the corner. You feel that your friends and family are getting on your nerves, and you can't wait to meet new people in college. You are tired of the rules that you have to follow and might even say something that I have heard so many Christian seniors say to me, "I am just tired of having to be 'good'!" Then, once you finally get to college, you allow this newfound freedom to exploit you and take you for a ride. In college, the distraction continues in the form of this freedom.

This distract, disconnect, and deceive move is the best trick that Satan has, and he has perfected it. As a matter of fact, he started out doing it pretty well. In Genesis 3, we see the first account of it. Here is how it began. God has created the world, and it's beautiful. He put two people on the earth and basically gave them permission to do whatever they wanted to do. They could walk around with God, name some animals, and just, as God put it, "become fruitful and multiply." There were thousands of food options, all fresh and at their disposal. They could do everything except eat from one particular tree. The tree of knowledge of good and evil, as it was called, was off limits and for good reason too. God wanted to protect Adam and Eve from knowing what evil looked like. It's hard to imagine this now, but there was a time when man did not know evil. Things like lying, cheating, and murder were not known because sin had not yet entered the room, and God wanted deeply to protect us from this. He knew that to disobey this command would open man's eyes to see a world that is forced to put good and evil in two separate corners of a fighting ring. Satan knew this too and was determined to "kill, steal, and destroy" the identity of mankind. His plan was to distract, disconnect, and deceive. Here is how it went down:

> Now the serpent was more crafty than any of the wild animals the LORD God had made. He said to the woman, "Did God really say, 'You must not eat from any tree in the garden'?"
>
> The woman said to the serpent, "We may eat fruit from the trees in the garden, but God did say, 'You must not eat fruit from the tree that is in the middle of the garden, and you must not touch it, or you will die.'"
>
> "You will not certainly die," the serpent said to the woman. "For God knows that when you eat from it your eyes will be opened, and you will be like God, knowing good and evil."

When the woman saw that the fruit of the tree was good for food and pleasing to the eye, and also desirable for gaining wisdom, she took some and ate it. She also gave some to her husband, who was with her, and he ate it. Then the eyes of both of them were opened, and they realized they were naked; so they sewed fig leaves together and made coverings for themselves. [17]

Did you see it? Satan convinced Eve that (1) God was holding out on them, (2) God was lying when He said that they would die, and (3) there was nothing wrong with the fruit on that tree. So they bought into the lie, ate the fruit, and ushered sin into the world.

Today, we do the same thing. Satan is at work in our culture and keeps knocking on the door of our lives to distract, disconnect, and deceive. He is determined to convince us that we are not worthy of the full life in Christ. He tells us that we are not good enough, smart enough, attractive enough, strong enough, or faithful enough for God. He convinces girls that they have to starve themselves to be beautiful. He tricks guys to think that an image on a computer screen is desirable and fulfilling. The dating couple thinks that they must have sex to show their love, and the fraternity pledge thinks that he has to compromise himself at a party to be liked. It's all a lie, and it is destroying our relationships and ourselves. It causes emotional, mental, physical, and spiritual wounds that remain open for years, all because we are still deceived to take the fruit.

PERSPECTIVE

How do you keep yourself from falling for the lies of spiritual identity thief? How can you go from here and stand strong as the person that you were created to be? For many, that means having to start from scratch because their identity in Christ has already been taken. For others, it is just a matter of protecting it from future harm. Either way, right now is the best time to begin.

This process of knowing who you are can be summed up in one word: perspective. Perspective is simply how you see things. In life, perspective is everything. Two people can see the same situation and come up with two completely different stories. A team of referees can see a play and make different calls. You can live your life one way and later realize how stupid your decisions were, all because you gained more perspective. Your perspective will vary by how you were raised, by the experiences you have had, and by how you allow culture to influence you. Self-perception is the perspective that you have of yourself. Having an accurate self-perception will save you from making many costly, poor decisions in college and the rest of your life.

As a follower of Christ, we are instructed to live our lives by Scripture. The Word is our compass for perspective. We believe that God's Word will give us the guidance we need to make decisions and give us the direction for our lives. It is when we veer away from Scripture that we convince ourselves that we are seeing things differently. You may say right now that there is no way that you will neglect your faith in college, but it doesn't take long to compromise your values when you allow yourself to view the world from a different perspective.

James 1:22-24 says, "Do not merely listen to the word, and so deceive yourselves. Do what it says. Anyone who listens to the word but does not do what it says is like someone who looks at his face in a mirror and, after looking at himself, goes away and immediately forgets what he looks like." This seems like an absurd example that someone would actually see his reflection in the mirror and then walk away and forget that image, but spiritually it makes a lot of sense. This verse shows us how directly connected perspective and self-perception truly are. If we are followers of Jesus, then our identity is found in Christ. That is who we are. Hearing the Word of God but not living it is forgetting who we are in Christ. When we forget who we really are, we form a false perception of ourselves. When our self-perception changes, our perspective changes. That is when we begin to think it is okay for us to say and do things that at one time we thought were wrong. At this time, we spiritually walk away from our true reflection, forgetting who we were created to be. That is why 3/4 of Christian high school seniors stop actively growing in their faith in Christ during their freshman year in college. They have lost their compass and the perspective that it gives.

Here are three perspective angles that will help you create a healthy self-perception so that you know who you are and can protect yourself from the spiritual identity thief.

1. **How does God see you?**

If our identity is to be found in Christ, then we must first understand how God sees us. The further we move away from an understanding of this, the more blurry the lines become of who we are and what we were made for. The truth is you were created to be in a relationship with God. God loves you deeply. In 1 Peter 3:18 we read: "For Christ also suffered once for sins, the righteous for the unrighteous, to bring you to God. He was put to death in the body but made alive in the Spirit." In this verse we see God's mission: to bring us to

Him. We were unrighteous, which means that we were not worthy to be in relationship with the God of the universe because of our sin. But Jesus became that sin so that we could know Him. Second Corinthians 5:21 says, "God made him who had no sin to be sin for us, so that in him we might become the righteousness of God." That is how God sees us, as righteous. He doesn't see us as the lonely, sinful, unworthy, incapable, insecure, unimpressive, worthless person that we sometimes see in ourselves. This is important to remember. Those typical self-perceptive characteristics that we convince ourselves are the makeup of who we are come from the thief and are opposite of how God really sees us.

A beautiful seven-year-old little girl that I know came home from school recently and told her parents that they didn't love her. She felt ugly and unloved. This broke my heart, not to mention her parents', who I know love her deeply. I know how indescribable it is to try to imagine the love a parent has for their child. I can't fathom the perspective that God has of us, that He would love us so much to give us life and life to the fullest. I think it breaks His heart when we allow the thief to convince us that we are anything other than the beloved righteousness of God.

2. How do others see you?

Once you understand how God sees you, you can begin to see how others see you. The difference is, our identity is found in Christ not in others, so understanding how others see us should only challenge us to be more like Christ. For example, I described that seven-year-old girl as beautiful, which she is. For some reason, even at her very young age, she didn't see herself as beautiful. But if she could understand that I see her that way, she might begin to see through the fog of her deception and understand who she truly is. This also works the other way around. If others see us as something other than the righteousness of God, knowing this might challenge us to prove them wrong by becoming more like Christ.

Alfred Nobel was a Swedish chemist who lived from 1833-1896. Throughout his life he held hundreds of patents, yet his most famous invention was dynamite. Even though he created the explosive material for a safer process of mining, it eventually became used for harm and violence. In 1886, Nobel's brother passed away, and the local newspaper mistakenly wrote an obituary for Alfred Nobel, rather than his deceased brother. The large headline read: "Le marchand de la mort est mort" ("The merchant of death is dead.") In the write-up, the newspaper wrote: "The merchant of death is dead. Alfred Nobel became rich by finding ways to kill more people faster than ever before."[18] After reading this, Alfred was devastated. Realizing what his legacy could become, he dedicated the rest of his life to peace. In 1895, he reconstructed his will to fund the Nobel Peace Prize, an award that spotlights individuals who devote their lives to further peace in the world. It wasn't until Nobel gained this perspective of how others saw him that he found his direction in life.

3. How do you see yourself?

The answer to this question will define who you become. If you believe the lie of the thief, then that is who you will become. Then your actions, decisions, and future will reflect that perspective of how you see yourself. We see this happen every day all around us, and we are so conditioned to it that we don't remember what it even looks like. It often begins with self-image. Your school is filled with beautiful, talented girls who see themselves as ugly, worthless people. The magazines have set a standard of who they should be, and they can't possible live up to that standard. As I write, Jennifer Lopez is the reigning People magazine's most beautiful woman in the world. Who can compete with that? If that is the standard, then there is not a girl at your school who can compete with J-Lo, because Jennifer Lopez (the person) can't even compete with J-Lo (the image). Lopez is also in the news right now because of her recent divorce with Marc Anthony. If being crowned the world's most beautiful woman was a healthy self-defining perspective, then why is her marriage falling apart at the same time? Living up to the standard of the world is not working for Jennifer Lopez, and it won't work for you either. Look at the athletes, actors, and rocks stars that we deem as successful, talented, and secure. Most of them suffer through life as unfulfilled because they have put their identity in everything except Jesus.

BECOMING THE PERSON GOD IS CALLING YOU TO BE

In 1 Samuel 7, we see that the people of Israel forgot that they were God's chosen, and they began to worship idols (not David Cook and Carrie Underwood, but rather Baal and Ashtaroth). They spent twenty years in idol worship, and let's just say, things weren't going very well (go figure). So Samuel told them that if they wanted to come back to God, they would have to put away the idols and serve God only. Then he said God would protect and restore them. So this is what they did. They got rid of the idols and committed themselves to worshiping and serving God. In return to this renewed faithfulness, God destroyed their enemy, the Philistines, and He restored peace in their land.

So many times we try to be someone we are not. We think that it will get us more friends, more attention, or a better life, but at some point, like the people of Israel, we realize that we have drifted away and no longer know who we are. At this point, we have two choices. One, we can think that we are too far gone and just walk farther away; or two, we can put aside the things that stand between us and God and go to Him. Then He will bring us peace. Not necessarily peace from war, like with the Israelites, but peace for our soul. In 1 Samuel 7:12 we read that to help them remember what God did, the Israelites placed a large stone called an Ebenezer and said, "Till now the Lord has helped us." This stone would help them remember that they were God's people. Sometimes we need something to help us remember who we were created to be.

In the fall of 2010, a seventeen-year-old girl who lived down the street from me died in a tragic car wreck. Her name was Virginia, and I can still picture her in my mind as a ten-year-old climbing a big tree in my front yard. She was such a great person, and it was so sad to see her life cut short. At her funeral, I saw hundreds of her teenage friends sitting there pondering life. They were all thinking about this friend that they had lost and were seeing life from a new perspective. I know from talking to some of Virginia's friends that her death changed their lives. Virginia saw her life through a Christlike perspective. She knew who she was in Christ, and that is why, when she died, her friends were forced to do a self-reality check, and many of them discovered who they were in Jesus, too.

As I said at the beginning of this chapter, God's story is the basis for your own story. Your story is the journey of your life as it relates to your relationship with God. Some people have amazing stories. You have heard of people who have overcome great conflict and changed the world. Others have had stories of struggles, unresolved issues, and broken relationships. Remember, your story relates to your relationship with Christ, and God's story is for all people, even if they don't believe in Him. So it would stand to reason that the determining factor in the success of your story comes down to the relationship that you have (or don't have) with God.

At your age, only a small part of your life story has been written. You could say that the stage has been set for the best part of your story to come. Some of your story, so far, has developed out of your control (where you live, who your family is, etc.). The older you get, the more influence and choice you have over your story. As you graduate and go to college, you will continue to write your story as you live your life. I believe that God has designed you for a purpose and has a plan for your life, and that He will open and close doors as He leads you through your story. I also believe, because I have seen it play out with so many friends, that to veer from God's plan is to stop living your God-ordained purpose. This choice is yours to make. God is inviting you to greatness in His eyes and in the lives of others, but you must decide who you want to be. Once upon a time, you were in your senior year in high school, and you realized that your life was on a path that would one day change the world …you finish the story!

Chapter Three
COLLEGE LIFE

Graduation had finally come and gone, and Justin was excited about going off to college. He had worked hard in high school to make good enough grades to go to the school of his dreams. During the summer he had stayed up many nights thinking about how it was going to be: what new friends would he make, who would be his roommate, and how hard would college be. Although Justin was not super-spiritual, he thought of himself as a good guy. He was nice to others, generous, and believed in God. In high school, Justin ran track, so he did not party very much. Occasionally, he would get drunk with his friends, but he was responsible and well-respected in his school. Once Justin got to college, he was ready to live life and have fun; he was away from home and ready to get his new life started.

Matt was Justin's new roommate. They did not know each other until orientation but hit it off and moved into the freshman dorm together. Matt too spent the summer thinking about what college would be like and was glad that the time had finally come. Matt grew up in a Christian home and felt sheltered from the world around him while in high school. He never got to go to the parties he heard *about and always wondered what it was like to be there.*

After Justin and Matt moved into their dorm room, they hung out and became close friends. A week into their new life as college freshmen, they met some of the older students and found out where the good parties were and who the "in-crowd" was on campus. A few nights later, Justin and Matt got wasted at a party and stumbled back to their room around 3:00 a.m.

"Man, that was fun," Justin commented as he fell into the bed.

"Yea," Matt responded as he thought about how bad he felt both inside and out. Matt felt bad, not just because he had too much to drink, but also because he did not like the guy he had become in just one night. As he thought about himself in high school as opposed to who he had been that night, he began to like "high school Matt" better. Before, he thought his life was boring, but now he was beginning to think it was more alive and free. Matt knew that this was just the beginning of partying with Justin and all of his new friends. Matt knew he had to make a choice. He knew his choice was to either hide his uncomfortable feelings toward this new potential lifestyle or to fall back on the faith he had and rest in it throughout his time in college. His options were clear, and he knew he needed to make a decision, and make it before the next party.

I graduated from high school in the early nineties and decided to go to a small liberal arts university. I remember finishing high school and being excited and scared at the same time about how my life was about to change. I was blessed to come from a strong Christian home with parents who loved God and taught me to follow Him. I was a pretty normal high school student, probably somewhat sheltered by living in my little "Christian bubble," but for the most part, typical. I liked sports but was always a second stringer, had a passion for music and was just learning how to use it, and loved making people laugh, which usually got me in trouble with the teachers. I never made great grades, not because I was not smart but because I really didn't see the money in it (plus, I was a slow reader because I often saw wrods and nubmers bcakwrads). So when it came to college, I was ready for the college life but a little nervous about the academics. I chose to go to my particular school because I had friends who were already going there. Plus, I wanted to go to a small school where I could be more than just a number.

I learned a lot in college, in and out of the classroom. For example, I learned how many rolls of Duct Tape it would take to construct a wall over a dorm room door, entrapping the person inside. I learned how hard you have to push on a sleeping cow for her to tip over (and what happens if you don't push hard enough). I learned the physics of how to effectively launch a water balloon out of a dorm window, over a large oak tree, across the quad, and into a group of sunbathing Chi Omegas. I also learned the depth of friendship that you can have when you live with your friends 24/7 and experience life together.

One of the best parts of being in college is living with friends. I have so many fun memories with my friends in college. The great thing about spending time with friends at college is that you don't always have to go out to have fun. Some of my best memories are about just hanging around in the dorm, the house, or the apartment where everyone lived. We would always hang around and talk, play Nintendo, or just goof off.

I was always up for a good prank or joke. We had lots of good ones (many of which I can't share in this book). I remember we used to play a phone game that would leave us laughing for hours. At my school, all of the dorms had specific phone number prefixes. This game was played before the days of caller ID and call return. Basically, the concept rested on the technology of three-way calling. Three-way calling works if you dial someone, and after they answer, you click the line to get a dial tone. Then you call someone else and click the line again to find all three people are on the line together. So we would call a random girl's number, and wait until she answered, and then say, "Hey ...hold on, I have another call." So before she figured out who had called her, she would be on hold. Then we would call a random guy's room. The moment the guy answered and said hello, we would click over and all be on the line. We never said anything else, and so they would begin to question each other. We would then listen to a series of "Who is this?" and "I didn't call you; you called me!" arguments. We actually had a few victims/contestants meet and begin dating because of the phone game.

College life is for moments like those. From fun, meaningless nights with the guys, to heartfelt discussions about life, God, and of course, girls—like building a house brick by brick, you will create lasting memories as you build them day by day. For me, college was a compilation of life experiences and lessons, but looking back on it now, at no time did I ever put a moment of thought into making a healthy spiritual transition. I just took things as they came and tried to make decisions based on my background and surroundings.

A WORLD ALL ITS OWN

Yesterday morning I was up early surfing … you know, the channels of the TV. I came across one of those nature shows that, while you're never interested enough to set the TiVo, you always have to stop and watch for a while during channel flipping. The show was about animals that live in clusters. It seems that monkeys, giraffes, elephants, and rhinoceroses, among many others, all live in herds basically for protection and safety. So as I'm sitting there, ironically, eating a box of animal crackers, and thinking about those animals that eat, sleep, and graze together, I begin to think about you and the next four years of your life.

Before we focus too much on college, let's take a moment and look back at high school. What did you learn about yourself in high school? How did those years prepare you for college life and adulthood? What would you say are the biggest differences between high school and college? Below, make a list of the differences you see in the following four categories:

Academically:

Socially:

Emotionally:

Spiritually:

As you can see, there are many differences in high school and college. Academically, the classrooms are larger in college, and the teachers are usually not able to devote the personal attention to you like a high school teacher. Socially, living with your friends, away from your parents, is a huge change that takes some getting used to. Emotionally, college is different because many college freshmen get homesick and miss the daily routine that they once had. Spiritually, college students have to be more mature about the decisions they make because they no longer have the Christlike influences around them that they once did. There are many more differences, and I challenge you to think more about them so that you can fully prepare for this next stage of your life.

College is a world of subcultures. Everyone fits into a group or a group of groups. Even those who are anti-group (and every college has them), they're a group, too. You have those in the Greek system, varsity athletes, student government, Christian organizations, dean's list, RAs, math majors, business majors, art majors, and of course the chess and backgammon clubs. If you don't believe me, look on any university website and you will see hundreds of groups to belong to. College is like a mini-country of learners and socialites. I guess you could make the argument that high school is a subcultural society as well, and in a way, you are right. But the main difference between the two is the rules. In high school, you live under a structured environment (home), go to a school that's structured (rule #1—you have to actually go to class), and for most people, live in a community that cares about you and watches over you (your home church, neighbors who have known you since you were five, etc.). In other words, the main difference between high school and college is freedom. There, I said it! The "F" word—freedom: that gift that you have waited all of your life for and the number one cause for why parents of college freshman spend sleepless nights worrying. If I had to describe the difference between high school and college in one descriptive word, it would be the word "more." College is everything that high school is but more. More people, more parties, more studying, more money (that is, it takes more money to be there), more time, more opportunities (good and bad), and of course, more freedom.

LET FREEDOM RING!

Remember the movie Braveheart? I love that movie! Every time I see it, I have a sudden yearning to paint my face, wear only a towel, and march around the house yelling really cool things. I can still hear William Wallace on the battlefield with his troop of ruffians as he is preparing them for battle, saying those famous words, "Just one chance to come back here and tell our enemies that you can take our lives, but you can never take our freedom!"[19]

When I ask my friends who have just graduated from high school about the one thing they are looking forward to most about going to college, the nearly unanimous answer is freedom. I can understand that. You have spent your entire life under your parents' roof. You have grown up with their rules and restrictions. Hopefully, they have taught you the difference between right and wrong, and now you are mature enough to experience a little bit of life on your own. But don't get too carried away.

What do you think is the normal tendency when someone experiences freedom for the first time? The majority of people take it one step at a time and slowly move into it, right? Of course not! Most people go wild and soak up as much as possible. As fun as that might sound to you after years of being supervised and chaperoned, it's not a very smart thing to do. For example, when you were a baby, did your parents go from feeding you from a bottle to giving you a buck and sending you out for a burger? No! They took you to the next level, which was baby food. Then, as you got older and matured, you were ready to have more solid foods. First Corinthians 3:2 says once you were a "mere infant in Christ. I gave you milk, not solid food, for you were not yet ready."[20]

Do you remember the day you got your driver's license? David, a friend of mine who just graduated from high school, told me about the day he went to take his driver's test. He got into the car with the instructor and, almost by instinct, sped off. He wasn't even out of the parking lot before the driving instructor told him to turn around because he had failed. David had to come back the next day and retake the test.

Anytime you blaze new territory in your life, you should be careful about jumping into it too fast. Why do you think that, in general, college life is so synonymous with wild parties, Spring Break on MTV, and Girls Gone Wild?[21] Just before you say, "I would never do that," let me tell you that I have personally known dozens of college freshman who graduated from high school with dignity, purpose, and a genuine longing for God who start college and within a couple of months become known as the life of the party.

I have never been much for alcohol. I did not grow up with it around my house as a child, and in high school I was smart, or naïve, enough to stay away from it, for the most part. I was one of those "morally good" Christian high school kids who chose not to party because of an image, not because of Christ. So as you can imagine, when I got to college I was confronted with alcohol at every turn. Lucky for me, I did not like the smell of beer so it was not a temptation to me, but ever since I was a kid, I have always loved fruit punch and fresh fruit. I can still remember in early September of my freshman year in college, I went to the first band party of the fraternity that I had just joined. At the party they had a huge cooler full of fruit punch with sliced oranges and apples in it. Now, I knew that there was alcohol in the punch, but when I was offered some, I partook. And I liked it. As a matter of fact, since I could not taste the alcohol, I figured that there could not have been very much in it. So, I had more. And then I had more. I'm not sure how much I had that night, but I know I made many visits to fill up the Big Gulp plastic cup I was using. The last thing I remember about that night was sitting on a bench with my head bowed and my eyes closed because that was the only way I could keep the world from spinning. I learned later that a friend took me back to the dorm and put me in bed.

As I look back on that day, I think that I really did not know what I was doing. I didn't understand the power of alcohol. The main thing I learned from that night was I knew that I did not like the way I felt. Sure the buzz was fun for a while, but the feeling that I was not in control of myself was scary. You could have asked me for all my money, and I probably would have happily given it to you. Ladies, I could have gone wherever with whomever and probably not have known the difference. The next day I got out my Bible and reread Ephesians 5:18, which says, "Don't get drunk with wine, because that will ruin your life. Instead, let the Holy Spirit fill and control you."[22] Before that night, I thought that verse said don't get drunk because drinking was wrong. That's not what it says. It says don't get drunk because if a substance is controlling you, God cannot. It was then that I understood that God is not about rules to be mean and take our fun away, but that He wants to deepen our relationship with Him by protecting us. It's like a parent telling a child not to play in the street when they live next to the world's greatest playground. Freedom is best used when you know how to control it. The only way to control the temptation of freedom is to be prepared before you are confronted with it. Just remember, a wrong decision is like a hidden turn on the highway. You don't know you're there until you've passed it.

WHY NOT JUST HAVE FUN NOW, WHILE YOU'RE STILL YOUNG

This is a concept that every generation tries to adopt as their own. The idea is that, while you are young, you can live carefree and then have plenty of time to live as you should when you're older. The truth that I've learned is that your human nature really does not change as much as you think it does as you get older. In other words, you don't grow out of your childhood character with age. When I was a teenager, I loved video games, loud music, and BBQ potato chips. Now I'm an adult, and guess what, I still love video games, loud rock and roll, and potato chips of the barbecue persuasion. The only difference is the games are better, the music will cause me to lose my hearing one day if I'm not careful, and the chips are still very, very good but appear to be more fattening than they were years ago. Here's my point. Many of the things you struggle with now will be around when you get older. The key to growing up is not getting older; it's getting wiser. And the older you get, the harder that choice is to make. I know adults who are in their thirties, forties, and fifties who act like children most of the time. They still cheat, lie, and act in the same immature way they did when they were twelve.

The story is as old as time. A twelve-year-old boy takes his first sip of beer. It tastes bad, but he likes it because his friends think he's cool. Then in middle school, he gets drunk for the first time. It makes him sick, but no one really gets hurt. In high school, this guy is drinking every few weekends. He's now moved on to heavy liquor and likes the attention he gets. He thinks that it probably is not that good for him, but he's young, so why not live it up while he can? In college, his once-a-weekend binge turns to four or five nights a week. He makes good grades and thinks that once he graduates he will have to tone it down some. Now he's out of school and has landed a great new job making lots of money. He works eight to five every day and parties Thursday through Sunday nights, drinking fewer nights but more at a time. By the time he's twenty-six, he's been through two jobs and four girlfriends. At twenty-eight he marries, but by forty he's divorced, struggles with keeping a job, is a lousy father, and is facing treatment for alcoholism.

Another guy likes to spend money. In college, he gets enough money from his parents that he is able to buy what he wants, take a date to the nicest of restaurants, and buy a round for all his friends when out with the guys. After graduation, he gets a great job making more money than a single guy could realistically spend. Twenty years later, he might live in the nicest neighborhood and drive a beautiful sports car, but his debt is more then he can bear, and his life falls apart.

These stories may sound extreme, but they happen to more people than you might think. Look at the divorce rate in this country. They say that one out of every two marriages ends in divorce. How many of those stem from an affair, neglect, abuse, or lies? I will give you a hint ...all of them! The abuse of freedom often begins in high school or college, but the world is full of adults who still take advantage of freedom and never realize that you do not grow up with age, but with wisdom.

Before you get any older and any further into your teenage years, start thinking about your choices and how they affect you. If you know your limits before you are tested, you will be much closer to making a better, wiser decision. Freedom is not a bad thing. If controlled, freedom can be fun, and ... well, freeing.

COLLEGE EXPECTATIONS

Every college freshman has spent hours thinking about what the college experience will be like. You have heard the stories, seen the movies, and talked to those who have been there, and you think you have a pretty good idea as to what college will be like. With that information, you form expectations about the next stage of your life. You wonder who will be your roommate, you dream of who might be your formal date, and you hope that you get a decent schedule and fair professors. If you are like me, you have rehearsed conversations and social scenarios in your head, and in the end you saved the day and got the girl/guy.

It's good to think about your future and develop expectations as you go. As I said in the introduction, some of your expectations might be close to the reality of college, but don't be surprised if you are way off. I have known lots of students who went away for college and returned home in a semester or in a year because their expectations were unrealistic, and, therefore, they had not prepared for a healthy transition. Take Ben for example. Ben graduated from high school at the top of his class. Plans of medical school brought him to college to major in chemistry. Ben was ready for college, so he thought. Ben's motivation for doing well in high school was driven by the pressure his parents put on him. When Ben moved to college, he assumed that making good grades would be as easy as it was in high school. Only there, he had a mandatory daily study hall at school, and his dad was always looking over his shoulder to make sure he studied at home. When Ben got to his first day of college classes, he found that the pressure to succeed was not there. As a matter of fact, there was not even a pressure to go to class. Ben found skipping class and staying up late at night with friends were his expressions of his newly found freedom. Ben's parents were surprised and highly upset to learn that Ben had flunked out of college his freshman year.

Having developed expectations for yourself in college is directly connected to having a successful result when college is over. As the old saying goes, "If you aim for nothing, you will surely hit it." Just before my wife and I got married, we went to pre-marriage counseling with our pastor. One of the first questions he asked us during the first session was to share our expectations of marriage. For the next few minutes, we each told what we thought our marriage would be like. It was an important step for us to share what we expected this new life of ours to be like. During any life transition, recognizing our expectations of the next step is important so that we can begin to picture ourselves doing well there. The main point I want to make in this chapter before we get into the core of this book is the importance of mental, emotional, and spiritual preparation before you get too deep into college. If you are already a freshman or sophomore in college, my hope is that as you read the rest of this book you will think about how you can make some changes to start fresh from where you are. Even Ben was able to come home for a year, go to a junior college to get his grades up, and transfer to another school to continue his trek toward medical school. A change can always be made at whatever stage of life you are in. The truth is that the sooner you make that change, the better off you will be.

COLLEGE MISCONCEPTIONS

As I said before, forming expectations is a natural preparation as you transition into college. As with any new experience, your expectations might not be completely accurate. I would like for us to look at some common misconceptions that many students have about college.

"I will never feel lonely living in a dorm." This is a very common misconception that would seem very logical to someone who has lived his entire life at home with the family. It is true that in college you live on a hall or in a house with more people, but it is different because, unlike living with your family, you do not know what makes your roommates tick or what might get them ticked. The fact is everyone feels lonely at times, even when surrounded by other people. You will get tired of them, and they will get tired of you. People disappoint people; it's a fact of life. But if you go in with a realistic expectation, you will be prepared.

Elizabeth and Meredith were on the cheerleading squad together in high school. They were together all the time, hanging out on weekends, double dating for prom, and even studying together for exams. So when they both decided to go to the same college, they made what they thought was a natural progression of their friendship by deciding to be roommates. Before starting college, they spent lots of time thinking of all the things they would be able to do together. To Elizabeth and Meredith, this was going to be more like a long-term slumber party, rather than just being college roommates. After a few weeks of living in the close quarters of a dorm room, Elizabeth and Meredith began to get tired of each other. They got on each other's nerves, and by the end of the first year, they were no longer roommates or very close friends. Their expectations of being best friends/roommates was crushed by the reality that they were too close to spend that much time together. If they could have done it over again, they would have each gotten a roommate and lived down the hall from each other. This choice would have given them each the opportunity to expand their base of friendships as well as would have allowed them to spend quality time together without smothering one another.

"There is a four-to-one ratio of the opposite sex; I am sure to find my soul mate." College is a great place to date. There are always things to do and more time to do them. Though many people find love in college, not everyone will. The danger of this expectation is that many people look so hard to find love in college that they end up settling for someone they really don't love. If growing in your faith is important to you, then you should only consider dating someone who has a similar passion for Christ. Second Corinthians 6:14-15 reminds us: "Do not be yoked together with unbelievers. For what do righteousness and wickedness have in common? Or what fellowship can light have with darkness …What does a believer have in common with an unbeliever?"[23] You may have heard the old saying, "Don't date anyone you would not consider marrying." If you seek a future spouse who is grounded in his/her faith, why would you consider dating someone who is not so?

Lisa is a friend of mine. In high school she was strong in her faith. When she went off to college, she continued to be a leader in various Christian organizations and had thoughts of going on to seminary after graduation. Then she met John. John was a good guy with a great personality. John was very popular and a star on the baseball team. It was not long into her junior year that Lisa fell in love with John. John came from a different background than Lisa. He had not grown up in a Christian home and thought that Lisa's faith was great for her but not for him. Two weeks after they graduated from college, John and Lisa got married. Though their two-year dating relationship was smooth, their marriage was rocky. Christ was not the center of their relationship, and they were divorced only two years later. (I will tell you how I met my wife later in this book, but the moral of my story is once you stop looking for your soul mate, that's when you find him/her.)

"Academically, college will be easier because I am typically only in class a few hours a day." As I have already said, there is a big difference, academically, between high school and college. It is said that "high school is a teaching environment in which you acquire facts and skills. College is a learning environment in which you take responsibility for thinking through and applying what you have learned."[24] It is true that in college, you take fewer classes at one time than in high school. A normal college class load is only four or five classes at a time. A typical semester-based college will offer a three credit hour class either for fifty-minutes on Monday, Wednesday, and Friday or for ninety minutes on Tuesday and Thursday. It would be a pretty normal schedule for you to only have classes from 9:00 a.m. to noon on Mon/Wed/Fri and 8:30-12:30 on Tues/Thurs. That schedule is totally different from what you have been accustomed to for the past twelve years of your life. Don't let this fact make you complacent. It is easy to think you can get by with studying less than you did in high school, and for some rare people this might be true. When I was in high school, my parents made sure that I did my homework. When I got to college, it was a whole different story. Not only were my parents not there to keep me on track, but my friends were usually in the next room playing games, watching a movie, and doing something more fun than studying for that history test. I was easily distracted and usually had to pull an all-nighter because of it. (Take it from me; the all-nighter is a really bad study skill.) The bottom line is to know yourself and know what it will take for you to succeed.

"Peer pressure was not a big deal for me in high school, so I don't expect to suffer from it in college." I hear many Christian high school students say this with genuine confidence. If you were not tempted in high school by your peers, a good question to ask yourself would be: Why weren't you? Was it because you had a strong friend structure that kept you from falling? Were you like me in that you did not party in high school out of respect for your parents and the fear of disappointing them? Was it because you were active in a Christian group or organization that kept you accountable and always offered you other options for activities to do on the weekends? For all of these reasons that may have made you immune from peer pressure in high school, I have a follow-up question: Are your high school friends, your parents, and your Christian mentors going with you to college? My guess is no. Exercise caution and wisdom as you meet new friends and venture into unfamiliar territory in college and have to encounter new social pressures that might make or break you socially and spiritually.

Emily was strong in her faith through her junior year in high school. She went to church regularly and even served in some Christian leadership roles in her school. Emily's best friend,

Sara, was a year older than Emily, so when Sara went off to college, Emily was starting her senior year in high school. Sara got into the regular party scene within the first few weeks of starting her freshman year. It wasn't long before Emily started driving up to visit Sara at college on the weekends. After only one visit, Emily found herself in a place where no one knew about her faith and leadership at home. Emily began to party with Sara at college almost every weekend. It wasn't long before Emily started not only getting drunk every weekend with Sara, but she also began sleeping with college guys she met at parties. Back home, Emily was able to wear her responsible Christian mask, but inside it was tearing her apart. She did not know what to do, how to stop, or even if she wanted to stop. Emily sought help, but once she graduated and went off to the same college the next year, her reputation as a party girl was already established. We will talk more about being a social Christian in a later chapter.

"There are so many Christian organizations on campus; I will certainly be stronger in my faith than I was in high school." Even though there are usually more Christian groups available to you in college than in high school, it is still up to you to be involved. And then, that does not mean that you will grow in your faith. We will discuss this in more detail in chapter six, but for now, know that this is a common misconception that can lead many to years of stagnated spiritual growth. Recently, I was talking to my friend Lucy, who is a junior at a major Southern university. When I asked her about this, she commented that she was surprised by how hypocritical college Christians were. She had thought that once students got older and more exposed to the world around them that they would grow in their faith as well. She added, "To my surprise, college Christian groups are not all filled with people striving daily after Christ!" I will add that like some adults in our communities and in our churches, Christianity serves only as a religion and as a status symbol for some college students, rather than as a relationship.

When preparing for a smooth transition into college, one must know the facts. Unrealistic expectations can be a real transition killer and can keep you from making college a true adventure. In the next section of this book, we will look at making a spiritual transition. Now that you have a clearer picture of where you are going and what to expect, hopefully you are starting to feel more prepared for the adventure ahead of you. I believe that if you learn to own your faith, you will not only make college an amazing experience, but you will set yourself up for making life a journey of faith and purpose.

TRANSFORM
SECTION TWO

Chapter Four
OWN YOUR OWN

Ryan sits in a café with four of his fraternity brothers reading and talking about God. It is the beginning of his junior year. Looking back on the past two years of college, Ryan shakes his head and describes starting college as a Christian like "swimming upstream." His friends agree and share that going against the tide of the culture is hard for anyone wanting to grow in his walk with Christ.

Ryan grew up in a Christian home. In high school he was involved in church and Young Life. Each week, he and some of his friends met in a small group Bible study and talked about life issues. But once Ryan started his freshman year in college, this accountability group was gone, the current of college life took him under, and he struggled to stay afloat.

In the fall of his junior year, fate caught up with Ryan, and he was arrested twice in one week for underage drinking. It was at this time that Ryan decided to quit playing around with life and begin getting serious about the faith that he had put on hold a few years before. Just one day after praying to God for growth, Ryan got an e-mail from his old

Young Life leader asking if he wanted to come on a Colorado ski trip and serve on a work crew. Ryan loved skiing and Young Life, so he went. During this trip, Ryan met and got to know several students who attended the same university. It was easy to see that they were growing in their faith while in college. He also had a chance to get away and reflect on his own life.

Ryan went back to school with a new perspective. As it turned out, God was also working on a few of Ryan's friends, and these guys found themselves wanting to grow in Christ together. They quickly became accountable to each other and began learning from one another. Now they meet weekly in a café, talk about their walk with Christ, and pray about how they can share Christ with their friends in the fraternity and how they can continue to own their own faith.

Let's play a game! I'll name two things, and you pick the best one. Ready? Cheesecake or broccoli? Porsche or Pinto? A movie with friends or doing homework? Caribbean vacation or math class? These choices might seem like no-brainers. It is true that most people would rather have cheesecake than broccoli. Some decisions, like these, are pretty easy to make, but there are many decisions that we face that will alter the direction of our lives. How will you make those decisions? How will you ensure that you are making the best decision you can? Do you approach it like one of the questions above and just go by what you want more, which looks better, or which one is easier? When we are facing a real, life-changing decision, often the easiest, best-looking choice is not the right one.

My friend Will grew up in a Christian family where he went to church regularly and had many supportive Christian friends. He was a high school athlete with a promising college football career awaiting him. When he got to college, he lost sight of God and started focusing more on himself. It wasn't long before his life began to spin out of control. Will started partying all the time, and after he got his girlfriend pregnant, he lost his dream of playing major college football. So where did he go wrong? Was it his college friends that led him to make bad decisions? Was his biggest mistake having sex with his girlfriend? Was it something else that led up to that? Will made a series of bad choices because he made one major wrong decision: he allowed himself to lose sight of his relationship with Christ. He didn't take the time to understand what it means to take ownership of his faith.

At your age, you are discovering that life is full of choices. You may have already had to make some serious life decisions, and chances are you regret some of them. As you branch out and explore life, I would like to give you some advice: If you use God as your guide in life, He will never fail you. I assure you that if you will consult Him before you make a decision, He will lead you down the right path. But I know what you are thinking, Come on, Tommy! What you are saying sounds great in theory, but it is not easy or practical. I mean, how do you expect that, in the moment of decision, I am going to take the time to ask and wait for God to answer? Well, that's a great question, and strangely enough, I am planning to discuss that in this chapter.

The biggest challenge in college for a Christian is making the transition spiritually. At the heart of this transition is a series of decisions that you will be faced with, and even without thinking about it, your reaction to those situations will determine your ability to stay focused on your relationship with Jesus. You are now facing a whole new world, and as you learn to live on your own, you will be forced to make decisions that will affect the rest of your life. That is why you must decide to take that challenge head on by learning faith ownership.

But what do I mean by "own your own faith"? Before you answer, let me ask you this question: how do you plan to avoid straying away from God while in college? Put a check by the correct answer(s) below.

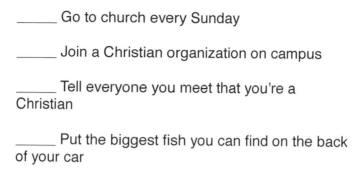

_____ Go to church every Sunday

_____ Join a Christian organization on campus

_____ Tell everyone you meet that you're a Christian

_____ Put the biggest fish you can find on the back of your car

How did you do? Do you think that you found the right answer? Well, the truth is that none of these four examples will guarantee that you will not drift away from your walk with Christ. There is no doubt that going to church, joining a Christian organization, and being honest with others about your faith are great ways to grow and keep yourself accountable, but the only way to guarantee that you will stay strong is to take ownership of your faith and develop a rock-solid relationship with God.

Early in my ministry career, I was asked by my mentor to chart my journey with Christ. This was something that I had never done before, and I knew it was going to be difficult. As I charted the strong and weak times of my faith, the graph looked like a diagram for the world's wildest roller coaster. After I had finished this outline from childhood to my mid-twenties, I learned something about myself that I had never thought of before. I learned that all of the times that I seemed to be at my strongest spiritually were the times when I was closest to those mentors and teachers in my life. The times with the most struggles were when I was away from them at school or just after I moved to a new place. The lesson that I learned from this test was that I need guidance in my life. While in college, I was not disciplined enough to carry on with my walk with Christ unless someone was looking over my shoulder. All of your Christian life you have had your parents, church and ministry leaders, teachers, or someone to keep you accountable for your walk with Christ. These friends and mentors were there to help you make good decisions and to steer you in the right direction. But, now you are older, and as a college student you will most likely live further away from those Christian influences from high school. How are you going to handle that?

When I was sixteen, I got a car. It was not a new sports car but, rather, a four-door 1983 maroon Oldsmobile hand-me-down from my mom. At first I was just glad to have a car so I could go wherever I wanted. I washed the car, had it checked regularly, and took good care of it. But a few years later, I became tired of the car and felt stuck with it. I stopped washing it and even went about six months without having the oil changed (I decided after it started leaving a half mile smoke trail, that I probably needed to take it in.). Now I have a car that I bought. It's still not the Motor Trend Car of the

Year,[25] but I bought it and paid it off. For the first time in my life, I have a car I can be proud of. I keep it washed and have it serviced every 3000 miles.

I hate to do yard work. I hated it as a kid, and I pretty much hate it now. Sometimes it's not that bad, but I live in the South where it is hot for most of the year. Nothing is worse than beginning to sweat just walking out the front door. When I was a kid, I had outside chores to do each week, which included cutting the grass (did I mention that I hated to do that?). My poor parents had to listen to me complain the whole time. Now, even though I still don't like mowing the grass, I take a weird sense of pleasure in it. It's still hot, and I'd still rather be doing something else. But the pride that I feel when I can look at how nice my yard looks makes it worth the trouble. The only difference in doing that chore as a kid and doing it as an adult is that it is my yard that I am mowing now. It's my house and my yard, to be enjoyed by my family. That makes all the difference in how I look at it and the quality of the job that I do.

The point is this: ownership comes with maturity, and you are more likely to care for something you own than something you are not solely responsible for. Owning your faith could be the hardest but most rewarding thing you will ever do for yourself. It is a significant move toward growing in a deeper relationship with Christ and making the spiritual transition from high school to college.

THE ANCIENT PATHS …

I want to give you part two of my college story. After that night at the party with all the fruit punch, I decided that drinking was not for me. I joined a popular fraternity and made it pretty clear from the beginning that my faith was important to me. For the next two and a half years, I lived my life the best that I could, trying to make the best decisions I knew how to make. I do regret many of the decisions that I made during those years, but for the most part, I felt like I did okay. Though I was unaware of it at the time, my spiritual life became stagnant during those years. I did not go to church very much unless I was home for the weekend, and my prayer life was virtually nonexistent. On the outside I was seen as the spiritual nucleus of my peer group. I was still the guy that people apologized to when they cussed, and friends of mine would offer me a beer with big grins on their faces, just to see what I would do. I served as the chaplain of my fraternity (a position that I created myself) and SGA chaplain my junior year. On the outside I was seen as Jesus, but on the inside I felt like the blind man of Mark 8.

The first two and a half years of college were growth-less years for me. Looking back, I can testify to the fact that God is always with you, even when you feel you are not with Him, and He always has a way of eventually bringing you back. The summer before my senior year, I got the opportunity to go on a mission trip to Russia. The trip was with Josh McDowell Ministries,[26] a subset of Campus Crusade for Christ. Mission to Russia '93, as it was called, was an amazing adventure. Josh McDowell —a well-known author, speaker, and in my opinion, modern Christian icon—had written a book called *More Than a Carpenter*[27] and traveled to Russia to preach and share the truth and hope of Jesus Christ. My job was to go out on the streets and pass out a Russian translation of More Than a Carpenter, which also included the Gospel of John. This trip was the perfect escape from my life and a chance to fall in love with Jesus all over again. While in Russia, I met many new friends and had many incredible experiences. During that trip, I discovered a verse that still stays with me today. The verse is Jeremiah 6:16, which reads, "Stand at the crossroads and look; ask for the ancient paths, ask where the good way is, and walk in it, and you will find rest for your soul."[28] Did you hear that —"rest for your soul"? What more could you ask for in a world that is always going, going, going, than to have rest for your soul? You know, your soul is like your spiritual self, and I can't think of anything worse than having a restless soul. God assures us that when we invite Him to be involved in our decisions and allow Him to guide us, then He will bless our souls with rest. It was that trip to Russia and this verse that helped me refocus and begin to take ownership of my faith. Jeremiah 6:16 is about the journey and the daily decisions we all have to make. God says when you stand at the crossroads of a decision, look around. Do you see any obvious signs to point you in a certain direction? Ask for the ancient path and the good way. I believe that your ancient paths represent all that God has taught you and prepared in you for this moment. This includes everything you have read, heard, and learned over the years about Jesus and His way. Through this process of prayer, you will find the good way, which is God's way, and then you will have to choose to walk in that direction. But when you finish that process, God will give you that needed rest. This verse could save your life; it saved mine.

...AND THEN GOD SENT UP A FLARE

Have you ever wished that you could have special super powers? You know, like Harry Potter, or better yet, like Luke Skywalker. I grew up in the Star Wars craze. I remember going to see the first Star Wars movie in the theater with my dad at the age of six. I used to pretend that I had the Force and would try to choke the family cat from across the room. The older I get, the more times I could use the help of Master Yoda to get me through situations and problems.

Life is a journey, but life can be hard. The journey has many paths, and sometimes decisions are hard to make. You might ask for the ancient path and the good way, but you still may not know which way to walk. You think if you could just know what God's will is, then you would know how to live. But if you are like me, you have had so many times in your life that you were not focused on God's way. There have been times in my life that I did not even know what it looked like, much less where to find it. Many times asking for the good way never crossed my mind, and I got so far away from the journey that I didn't know which way was north. And then God sent up a flare ...a sign ...a message ...a clue.

What if God is giving us a way to know His will? What if it is a clue within the journey itself? I think it is, and I want to share it with you now. Hang on because this one verse contains the very process of owning your faith. I believe that if you can know the value of this verse, and live out its meaning, you will walk the good path, the path that leads to your purpose in life.

Romans 12:2 says, "Do not conform any longer to the patterns of this world, but be transformed by the renewing of your mind. Then you will be able to test and approve what God's will is—His good, pleasing, and perfect will."[29] That's it, the key to owning your faith and the way to a healthy spiritual transformation!

Let's unpack this for a moment. This verse is a two-step process to faith ownership. First, it says to stop conforming to the patterns of the world. The word "conform" means to be or look similar to. In other words, it means to resemble the image of the world. It's like when a kid dresses up on Halloween. He's not actually becoming a Power Ranger when he pulls the famed red, blue, or yellow mask over his face (though he might think that he has), rather he has simply conformed to the image of the morphed superhero. Another translation of this verse says, "Don't copy the behaviors and customs of this world."[30] When I think about college students in this country as a whole, I think about world conformity. In part, I would say that it's not even all their fault. Turn on the TV for only a moment, and you will see that the media and advertising community spend billions of dollars targeting high school and college students and convincing the greater public what the world looks like.

"Hello, my name is Tommy McGregor, and I am a reality TV junkie!" I admit it; it's true. But at least I'm not alone …my wife is too (as is the rest of America, it seems). We love reality shows. I am not sure what it is about that genre of entertainment, but it seems that over the past decade more and more reality shows have become …well, a reality.

For me, I like the ones that are built around a competition like *Survivor*[31] and *The Voice*.[32] Other people might prefer those that follow people around as they live their "regular lives." Either way, each week, millions tune in to watch as normal people do crazy things for fame and a million dollar check.

Decades before reality television existed as we know it, there was a show called Putting on the Hits.[33] Even in the mid-1980s, *Putting on the Hits* was a Saturday evening must-see-TV moment for me. During this thirty-minute mega hit, real people would dress up like their favorite singer, develop a performance routine, and lip sync to a popular song. It was great! I was a twelve-year-old rock star wannabe, and Putting on the Hits was my answer. I remember watching these people become almost exact replicas of the artists they were imitating. I spent many nights in front of the bedroom mirror with a brush as my microphone as the radio blared my song. I was someone else; I was conforming.

We live in a world where it's hard to determine reality. We are accustomed to seeing airbrushed pictures of models and regular people living in "real" scenarios like forming alliances on remote islands surrounded by cameras. We live near people covering up their hardships and sufferings, pretending to be doing great, and then surprising everyone when the truth finally comes out. On the surface, our worldly nature tells us to pretend to be something that we are not, but God is asking us to become who we were created to be. Step one of knowing God's will for your life is to stop conforming to the image of the world.

Step two is to start transforming. It says rather than conform to the world, "be transformed by the renewing of your mind." To be transformed means to completely change from one thing to another. One of the great action movie series over the past few years has been *Transformers*.[34] But before the on-screen battles between the Autobots and Decepticons, some of the best toys ever made for boys were Transformers Action Figures.[35] I played with Transformers when I was young, and kids today still play with them (except now they are way better). The deal with a Transformer is that it looks like a regular vehicle, perhaps like a dump truck. The dump truck can roll around and dump things out of the back and basically operate in a semi-stealth disguise to hide its true mission. But once the world invasion begins, the unpretentious dump truck transforms into a mean fighting machine with cannons, armor, and, strangely enough, the back of a dump truck. The toy transforms from a truck to a robot. Once it is a robot, it no longer has the shape, form, or look of a truck.

To transform means to change. If you are living your life like the world says to live it, you will never know what God's will is for your life because the distractions of the world are too loud to hear

God speak. You must transform by the renewing of your mind. This mind transformation is a life-long pursuit. When you ask Jesus to come into your life, He comes into your heart and takes up residence. That's a done deal. Once He's there, He ain't moving! But once God is in your heart, it is up to you to put Him in your mind and keep Him in your mind. "Then," the Bible says, "you will be able to test and approve what God's will is." Another translation says, "Then, you will know what God wants you to do, and you will know how good and pleasing, and perfect His will really is."[36] You see, the goal of knowing how to own your faith is spending your life getting to the word "then." Once you can test and approve God's will for your life, then you can make a life transforming transition.

In this conquest over world conformity, you will find a new kind of freedom as you learn God's will and purpose for your life. Galatians 5:1 says, "It is for freedom that Christ has set us free."[37] This daily act of transformation originates in every decision that you make.

One of my favorite stories in the Gospels is the prodigal son in Luke 15. Jesus tells of the younger of two sons who asks and receives his share of his wealthy father's estate. It says that he cashed it in and moved to a foreign land and wasted all of his inheritance on "wild living." Once his money ran out, he got the only job he could find, which was tending to pigs. Then, in verse 17, what happens to the son is something that must take place in all of us before we can turn from conforming to transforming our lives. It says, "He finally came to his senses …" It's like he woke up, or maybe God knocked him on the head, but it said that he "came to his senses." You know the rest of the story. He goes back home and asks his dad if he could work for him, rather than be his son again. His father slaps him around a few times … No! His father gives him a big hug, puts a ring on his finger, and throws a huge party.[38] When you stop conforming to the world and begin to transform your mind, it's like you come to your senses and run home to Jesus.

Do you remember my friend Will that I told you about earlier in this chapter? It took him a while to grab this concept of faith ownership. After he got his girlfriend pregnant, he dropped off the football team and quit school for a while. He moved back home and got a job. By the time his daughter was born, he had broken up with that girlfriend but committed to be a responsible father. It was this situation and moving home that led him to begin taking ownership of his faith. He reconnected with a mentor from high school and started growing again in his relationship with Christ. He transferred to a smaller school in the same city where I live, and that is when I met Will. He started volunteering with the ministry that I worked with and was great with the teenagers in our group. He was a starting football player and lived in a community of other believers where he could grow and learn. Now, Will is married and playing semi-pro football. He is doing very well and has dreams of working with inner-city kids and helping them keep away from making some of the same mistakes that he did. Some might think that real living is a life outside of an active, growing relationship with Jesus, but truthfully (and you never understand this until after it happens) real life doesn't begin until you begin to take your walk with Christ seriously and learn how to own your own faith.

Chapter Five
WORDS OF WISDOM

Sarah says she can't remember a time when religion wasn't a part of her life and family, but it was more a head thing than a heart thing during high school and college. Faith and God were terms to be defined and memorized much like poetry, but not a heart-felt, emotional, life-changing experience. Sarah admits that she was content to be a moralist, always doing the right thing out of fear of being caught. She felt the pressure to uphold the "good girl" image that she had worked so hard to establish.

In college, Sarah met Brandon and they began dating. Brandon was Sarah's first serious boyfriend, so when Sarah fell for Brandon, she fell hard. Within a few weeks, Sarah and Brandon began to become intimate, and Sarah felt like her whole moral life was shattering. Sarah says that losing her virginity was the most damaging thing because that was something she had pledged to herself that she would not do. She found that getting over this situation and learning to trust and forgive herself and others, was the hardest part. Sarah says about her experience, "My moralist belief system failed me, and my previously righteous self found me in a world of unrighteous sin. Falling hard off the pedestal that I and the people surrounding me had created for myself, I was broken. Coming from a place where you've convinced yourself and everyone else that you are incapable of sin, temptation is a very powerful and overwhelming thing."

Through it all, Sarah says that God was with her. She can look back on it and see how God tried to guide her away from the situation and protect her. Sarah learned that Jesus is always there in your life. She has learned to trust Him and knows that the deeper her relationship gets with Christ, the easier she can see the roadblocks and open doors in her life. Sarah says about her journey, "I feel like every single event that has happened in my life has taken place for a reason. Every experience and every person has changed me and impacted my life to mold me into the person I am today. I am still learning (and struggling) often, but I know He prunes the ones He loves, so I anticipate with great joy the fruit that He has planned for me."

Want to hear a joke? Once, a mountain lion ate an entire bull for dinner. After he was full, the lion started roaring and kept roaring until a hunter heard him, snuck up from behind, and shot him. The moral of the story: when you are full of bull, keep your mouth shut! You know, what's almost as gut-wrenchingly hilarious as this joke is the truth that can be found in its words. Everyone, it seems, is full of "good" advice. I've heard it said that opinions are like feet; everyone has them and most of them stink (I think that is how the saying goes!). We live in a world that is full of fast information. Once something happens anywhere, people often know about it everywhere within moments. Thanks to blogs, text messaging, and social media sites, information gets passed around so quickly that we might hear it and never think to ask if it's true or not. The entertainment world tells us one thing; advertisement and the media tell us another; and your friends and parents say something altogether different. Who are you going to believe?

As a college freshman, you are old enough to begin making decisions on your own but still too young to know how to use wise judgment and reason. This is not meant to be an insult to your pre-adulthood status, but rather a fact of an obvious reality. Even in the working world, a term for someone messing up who is new to the system is referred to as a "freshman mistake." The chorus from the mid-1990s pop song "The Freshman" by Verve Pipe sums up this sentiment:

For the life of me I cannot remember,
What made us think that we were wise and we'd
never compromise,

For the life of me I cannot believe, we'd ever die for
these sins,
We were merely freshmen. [39]

101

In the last chapter, we looked at Romans 12:2. We learned about God's two-step program for knowing His will. Now that we know not to conform and to begin a transformation, we can begin thinking about the right way to start renewing our minds for Christ. But how? We must have some sort of gauge by which to measure the difference between conforming and transforming.

THE WISDOM FILTER

I have never been a very mechanically minded person. In other words, I can't fix anything. If something breaks around the house, I try to be the man, get the tools, and work on it until finally my wife pushes me out of the way and makes the repair. One time I actually used four tools to put together a grill that claimed to be, oddly enough, a "no tools required" job. Even though I'm a non-handyman, I have replaced an air conditioner filter a few times in my life. The task is pretty easy, and the result is very important. Basically, an air conditioner filter works to keep dust, pollen, and bacteria from circulating throughout your house. This way, you keep the air clean by filtering out the dirt.

What if you had a spiritual filter that you could run all decisions through before you had to make them? Wouldn't that be a great thing? Before having to decide if you are going to go out with this person, you filter that decision and see what comes out on the other side. If you have a relationship with Jesus, you have such a filter. As I said in the introduction, Jesus desperately wants to know you and be involved in your life. This wisdom filter is needed as you ask for the ancient path and the good way. Jesus says, "I will ask the Father, and He will give you the Counselor, who will never leave you. He is the Holy Spirit, who leads you into all truth. The world at large cannot receive Him because it isn't looking for Him and doesn't recognize Him. But you do, because He lives with you now and later will be with you."[40] And Paul writes, "Therefore be careful how you walk, not as unwise men but as wise, making the most of your time, because the days are evil."[41] You and I may not always know what the ancient path and good way is, but the Holy Spirit does, and He will lead you there if you will follow.

WHAT IS WISDOM REALLY?

We often relate wisdom to age. "A wise old man once told me ..." When you say this, people usually stop what they are doing and listen. Why? Because we equate wisdom with age. Remember in chapter three, I said that I know many older people who are not any wiser than they were as

103

teenagers. The reason is that age does not make you wiser; wisdom does. The filter of wisdom is from God. You are in school to gain knowledge, but you will go further in life if you gain wisdom as well. If you look up the word "wisdom" in a dictionary, you find that wisdom is simply a component of being wise and, furthermore, a synonym of knowledge. But I know lots of smart, knowledgeable people who do not exude wisdom. I would like you to look at a more spiritual definition of wisdom. In Freshman: The College Student's Guide to Developing Wisdom, Mark Matlock defines wisdom as "the human capacity to understanding life from God's perspective."[42] I like this definition because true wisdom comes from God. Proverbs says, "By wisdom the Lord founded the earth; by understanding He established the heavens." In other words, man thinks in terms of knowledge and information. God thinks with wisdom and understanding. If we are going to gain a godly understanding, we must pursue wisdom.

Happy is the person who finds wisdom and gains understanding. For the profit of wisdom is better than silver, and her wages are better than gold. Wisdom is more precious than rubies; nothing you desire can compare with her. She offers you life in her right hand, and riches and honor in her left. She will guide you down delightful paths; all her ways are satisfying. Wisdom is a tree of life to those who embrace her; happy are those who hold her tightly.[43]

If wisdom is our understanding of life from God's perspective, we must determine what God's perspective is. When the *Harry Potter and the Deathly Hallows: Part Two* movie came out, I went to see it with my wife. She is a big Harry Potter fan, and since this was the last movie of the famed saga, I watched all of the other movies the week before this last movie released so that I could share the experience with her. Throughout the movie, I was on the edge of my seat, just waiting to see what was going to happen next. "Was Harry gonna defeat Voldemort, and would he survive?" That was the looming question as I watched the story unfold. My wife, on the other hand, was experiencing the movie in a completely different way. You see, she had read all the books multiple times, and so she knew what was about to happen and how the story would end. As a matter of fact, she had such a knowledge of the story that, still to this day, she has a much better understanding of the overall story from beginning to end than I ever will. This is similar to how God sees our life. His perspective is larger and more knowledgeable than ours. God sees our life from beginning to end and yet can still grasp each and every detail. He sees the big picture, when all we can see is the day to day. The first step of wisdom is excepting God's perspective and prevision of our life. This wisdom will give us a better understanding of our life and an enhanced perspective of our future.

GAINING WISDOM

When I think about wisdom, I remember the story of King Solomon. Solomon is considered the wisest man to ever live, but not because he was born that way. Solomon was the son of King David. You remember David, the boy who killed the giant Goliath with a slingshot and a few rocks? Well, David grew up to be Israel's greatest King. It is said that David was a "man after God's own heart."[44] So when David died, his son Solomon took over the throne. One night God appeared to King Solomon in a vision, and said,

"What do you want? Ask, and I will give it to you!"..."Give me an understanding mind so that I can govern your people well and know the difference between right and wrong. For who by himself is able to govern this great nation of yours?"

The Lord was pleased with Solomon's reply and was glad that he had asked for wisdom. So God replied, "Because you have asked for wisdom in governing my people and have not asked for a long life or riches for yourself or the death of your enemies, I will give you what you asked for! I will give you a wise and understanding mind such as no one else has ever had or ever will have."[45]

Solomon became the wisest man in the history of the world and still was able to achieve great wealth, a long life, and death to his enemies.

So how do you gain wisdom? Like Solomon, you ask for it. James 1:5 says, "If you need wisdom, if you want to know what God wants you to do, ask Him, and He will gladly tell you. He will not resent your asking."[46] The daily use of wisdom will save you from a lot of hard times and heartache in your life. In the book The Best Question Ever,[47] Andy Stanley describes that the best question you could ever ask yourself in any given situation is: "Is this the wise thing to do?"[48] He describes this question as a lifesaver and pledges that "your greatest regret could have been avoided had you asked the Best Question Ever and then acted on your conclusion."[49] As I've stated earlier, you may have already had to make some hard decisions in your life. There is no doubt that you will be faced with many more extremely difficult decisions in the years to come. The difference between the wise and the unwise is how you will handle these decisions.

Mike grew up in a Christian home, and when he went to college he was a virgin, with plans to save himself for marriage. Mike had been taught in church and through the model relationship of his parents that sex was reserved for the bonds of marriage. Never having to deal with the pressure of having a serious girlfriend in high school, Mike's commitment to his future spouse had not been tested until a few weeks into his freshman year of college. That's when Mike met Catherine. Catherine was a very attractive girl who had been sexually active in high school and did not have the moral upbringing that Mike had. Mike's first unwise decision was to get involved with someone who was not a Christian and had a different moral stand on sex. It wasn't long before they began to experiment sexually, but Mike still said that he would not have sex before marriage. About a month into their relationship, Mike and Catherine fell in love. They spent more time together, and as their love grew, so did the temptation to have sex. It wasn't long before compromise began to soak through Mike's stand on abstinence, and he downgraded his stance from no sex until marriage to no sex before a commitment of love (unwise decision number two). On their six-month anniversary, Mike bought Catherine a ring. It was not an engagement ring but a ring of commitment. It was that night that they had sex for the first time because Mike had tricked himself into thinking that the feelings of love he had for Catherine were adequate expressions for sex and confused those feelings with the deep, life-committing love found only in marriage. Within two months of having sex, Mike and Catherine broke up.

THE TWO D'S OF WISDOM

There are a lot of words that I don't like that start with the letter D. Diet, for example, is not a fun word to me. Most people would agree that divorce is never a happy topic to bring up. Death is usually a sad thing to talk about. There are a lot of other really negative D words such as dentist, disaster, and dandelions, but one of the worst has to be the word "discipline." I don't like discipline in word or deed. The biggest reason is because discipline takes a lot of work and is usually unpleasant. As much as I dislike having to discipline my children and receive discipline from God, I love the idea of being self-disciplined. When I see highly disciplined people, I am in awe. A disciplined person is one who is focused, gets things done, and does it well. I want to do that …in theory. The road to self-discipline is life long. You are never fully disciplined. It is always a work in progress.

To gain wisdom, you must develop self-discipline. Like an athlete, you can never reach your goals if you don't put in the work. In 1 Corinthians 9:24-27, Paul describes discipline this way:

> Do you not know that in a race all the
> runners run, but only one gets the prize?
> Run in such a way as to get the prize.
> Everyone who competes in the games goes
> into strict training. They do it to get a crown

that will not last, but we do it to get a crown that will last forever. Therefore I do not run like someone running aimlessly; I do not fight like a boxer beating the air. No, I strike a blow to my body and make it my slave so that after I have preached to others, I myself will not be disqualified for the prize.

If I had to guess, wisdom is not on the forefront of the minds of most college freshmen. I can understand that, because it wasn't on my mind when I started college. Most teenagers think that wisdom is something that comes to older adults after they have learned all the lessons of life. So how, you might ask, can wisdom make a difference in my life right now? As we have already noted, college is a very social time in your life. When you graduate from college, you will leave that place with much more than a sheet of paper to hang on a wall. You will most likely leave college with good friends that you will have for the rest of your life, but the quality of those friends will be based on the wise decisions that you make along the way. Proverbs 13:20 says, "Walk with the wise and become wise, for a companion of fools suffers harm." Maybe you have heard the saying, "You are the company that you keep." Wisdom will play a key role in the type of friends that you make and, therefore, the experiences that you have with those friends in college. Proverbs 19:20 says to "Listen to advice and accept discipline, and at the end you will be counted among the wise." I want you to learn wisdom because since college, I have pursued wisdom at all costs, and as I look back on my life, I can see the effects of that pursuit. I now make decisions that make sense. I have friends who are wise, and I learn from them and grow wiser. Most importantly to me, I married an extremely wise women. This was not an attribute I knew to look for in a mate in college, but thankfully God knew what I needed most.

Another important part of gaining wisdom is learning to use discernment. Discernment is the ability to look at two options and decide (or discern) which is the right choice. There are worldly answers on how to best do this. You could use your experience to base a decision on. You could find a few friends and make a collective discerning decision, or you might think back to that episode of Dr. Phil and try to remember what he advised to do. Anyone of those methods will lead to an answer, but will they lead to the right answer? Using the wisdom filter and discerning, according to the direction of the Spirit, is the only way that you will make a truly right decision.

Again, in his book *Freshmen*, Matlock states, "The ability to effectively discern how things are impacting us and how we are impacting others relies heavily on our ability to understand the relationship that exists between causes and effects.

There are certain activities that God says will improve our lives and others that He declares will cause us to lose joy. The world chases many different goals than we do, and so this point of reference is important if we are to remain in alignment with God's perspective."[50]

One day wise King Solomon was visited by two prostitutes. They explained that they lived in the same house and both had recently given birth to baby boys. One of the women told the king that the other woman had accidentally killed her son by laying on him while sleeping. She then claimed that the woman got up and switched the dead baby for her healthy one, while she was asleep.

Then King Solomon said, "This one says, 'My son is alive and your son is dead,' while that one says, 'No! Your son is dead and mine is alive.'"

Then the king said, "Bring me a sword." So they brought a sword for the king. He then gave an order: "Cut the living child in two and give half to one and half to the other."

The woman whose son was alive was deeply moved out of love for her son and said to the king, "Please, my lord, give her the living baby! Don't kill him!" But the other said, "Neither I nor you shall have him. Cut him in two!"

Then the king gave his ruling: "Give the living baby to the first woman. Do not kill him; she is his mother."[51]

Solomon prayed for wisdom and got it. He then had to use it to rule over God's people, and he did so very well. The last verse of this account in 1 Kings 3:28 says, "When all Israel heard the verdict the king had given, they held the king in awe, because they saw that he had wisdom from God to administer justice."

Wisdom is a tool for making right choices. Making wise decisions is the key to living a life that is transformed in Christ. In the end, it's not about how many verses of the Bible that you know or how many nice things you do for other people. The one thing that will determine how well you lived your life will be how wisely you chose.

"Stand at the crossroads and look; ask for the ancient paths, ask where the good way is, and walk in it, and you will find rest for your soul" (Jeremiah 6:16). The difference between the wise and the unwise is in the asking, the looking, and the finding.

Chapter Six
THE WITNESS PROTECTION PROGRAM

Joe gets out his Bible, a pen, and notebook. "What am I going to say?" he asks himself. "I've never shared my testimony in public before." Joe is nervous because he has been asked to share his story at the weekly worship event on his college campus. Joe is happy that he has been asked because he knows he has a good story to tell. He knows that there will be some people there that night that need to hear what he has to say. He's just not sure quite how to start.

Joe came to college from a broken, non-Christian family environment. He always thought that Christians were weak and condemning of others. Within a few weeks of starting college, Joe was invited to a weekly worship event just down the street from where he was living on campus. He noticed that some of the other students who were going were not what he would think of as "typical Christians." They were cool kids who seemed to care about him even though they did not know each other. There seemed to be something different about their lives, something that Joe knew he did not have. Simply, those guys seemed secure.

So Joe went to the worship event and sat in the back. Keeping his head down so as not to be recognized, Joe watched as the rest of the crowd sang. The band that led the worship was good, and Joe wondered why he had not heard of them before in the local bar scene. After the music, a guy slightly older than the rest got up and talked about Jesus. The speaker was funny, interesting, and spoke of a God unlike any god Joe was familiar with.

After the guy spoke, some of the guys that had invited Joe got up, and one shared his testimony. This guy told about his life before having a relationship with Jesus, and strangely enough, it sounded a lot like Joe's life. Then he told how Jesus came into his life and made him a new creation. Now Joe was interested. He thought that this life the guy was describing sounded like real life. Joe was tired of living for himself. He wanted to be a new creation. He wanted to be like that guy up front. He asked Jesus into his life that night.

Back in his room, Joe picks up his pen and begins to write out his story. He prepares his testimony for the worship event and prays that the guy down the hall that he invited will come to hear what he has to say.

Living out Romans 12:2 is a daily effort. Don't think that you wake up the first day of college and decide, "Today I will stop conforming and start transforming!" Unfortunately, it is not that easy. Rather, you wake up every morning and ask for wisdom and guidance through the day. You pray that God will show you the ancient paths and the good way. Paul writes in Ephesians 4:

> *Since you have heard all about Him and have learned the truth that is in Jesus, throw off your old evil nature and your former way of life, which is rotten through and through, full of lust and deception. Instead, there must be a spiritual renewal of your thoughts and attitudes. You must display a new nature because you are a new person, created in God's likeness, righteous, holy, and true.*[52]

In 1970, the United States Congress passed the Organized Crime Control Act, which started the witness protection program. Since this time, almost 10,000 people have been relocated to an undisclosed location, given a new identity, and allowed to start their lives over.[53] These individuals are put into this protective environment because their old life was in danger, usually due to a convicting testimony against an infamous criminal. The US Marshal's job is to secure these protected individuals, give them the new identity, and protect them in their new life. The protected person and their family receive new names, housing, and jobs, all with official documentation and a made-up life history to ensure their safety.

Before you get too settled into your new life in college, I hope that you will enter a witness protection program, of sorts. Not that you will go into hiding, but rather just the opposite. In this type of witness protection, you recognize that it is time for you to act like the new person described in Ephesians 4. You begin to ask yourself, "How will I live in a world that I have vowed not to conform to?" College will be a very full and amazing chapter in your life, but living your life in Christ is the only way to fully live the life that you were created for.

LIVING IN A WORLD WITHOUT CONFORMING TO IT

For almost two decades, I have worked with teenagers. I love to go to the schools to hang out with my high school friends in the lunchroom. Most of the time, I am able to move around to different lunch tables and see a lot of people in thirty minutes. Sometimes between classes I walk down the halls of the school to see my friends before their next class. As comfortable as I am walking the halls of a high school, I am still aware that I am not a high school student. I'm younger than some of the teachers and administrators, but easily twice the age of the students. When I am on a high school campus, I am in the world of the teenager. To those who don't know me, I stick out like a sore thumb, but to others, I am a daily fixture in their environment. Though I'm not a teenager, I am accepted for who I am—someone who cares deeply about them and wants to be their friend.

When you go to college with total ownership of your faith, you will live in a world that is different from yours. You will eat, sleep, study, and socialize in an environment of people who will not have the same moral goals as you have. How will you handle that pressure? How will you live in a world that you have vowed not to conform to? What will you say when someone asks you to do something that will compromise your commitment? The best answer I can give to that question is to pray and stay ahead of the game. In Following Jesus: A Non-Religious Guidebook for the Spiritually Hungry, author Dave Roberts asks the challenging question, "Can we be in the world but not of it? Jesus, even as He prepared for the cross, prayed to the Father, 'My prayer is not that you take them out of the world but that you protect them from the evil one.'"[54] If a prayer of protection is good enough for Jesus, it is good enough for you and me.

I still, to this day, wake up every morning and ask God to guide me and direct my every move. I try to pray myself away from temptation and toward opportunities to let my light shine. This is my daily prayer! I also try to see obstacles before they come at me. In college I tried to plan out what I would say and how I would act before I had to say and act on it. This got better with practice, plus I learned that once my close friends knew my stand on certain issues, it became easier and more accepted. As you make the transformation, you will begin to see your heart change, too. Galatians 5:16-17, 22-23 says,

> So I say, let the Holy Spirit guide your lives. Then you won't be doing what your sinful nature craves. The sinful nature wants to do evil, which is just the opposite of what the Spirit wants. But the Holy Spirit produces this kind of fruit in our lives: love, joy, peace, patience, kindness, goodness, faithfulness, gentleness, and self-control.[55]

The fruit of the Spirit is the outgrowth of a faith transformed. With these fruits in your life, you will be seen as different to the world because you will be different from the world. The result of a life lived by the fruit of the Spirit is one that makes a difference in others. When you live your life in this way, you will naturally influence those around you in the name of Christ. The rest of the world is anything but love, joy, peace, patience, etc. When you exhibit these qualities, you become what Jesus called salt and light. In Matthew 5:13 Jesus says, "You are the salt of the earth. But what good is salt if it has lost its flavor? Can you make it salty again? It will be thrown out and trampled underfoot as worthless." This might sound like a strange thing for Jesus to compare us to, but when you know the real purpose of salt, it begins to make sense. Even though we use salt mainly for flavoring our food, salt's main purpose is to preserve. Back in the days before refrigerators, if you had some meat, you would cover it with salt to keep it fresh before cooking. You could say that salt keeps food from going bad. As the salt of the earth, you and I are called to preserve those around us by showing them an example of Christlikeness.

Jesus then continued to say in verses 14-16:

> *You are the light of the world—like a city on a hilltop that cannot be hidden. No one lights a lamp and then puts it under a basket. Instead, a lamp is placed on a stand, where it gives light to everyone in the house. In the same way, let your good deeds shine out for all to see, so that everyone will praise your heavenly Father.*[56]

There is a Young Life camp in north Georgia called Sharptop Cove.[57] It is a great camp that I have been to many times. The camp is in a valley surrounded by the Georgia mountains. On the top of the mountain, overlooking the camp are some houses. These houses are on the side of the mountain maybe 500 feet up. At night you can look up and see the lights of these houses shining down on Sharptop Cove. From the vantage point of the camp, there is no way that those houses can have their lights on and not be seen from camp at night.

If we are to be that city on a hillside, we are going to be seen. As Matthew 5:14 continues to say, we are not to put something over our light to hide it. This is what Romans 12:2 refers to as "conforming to the patterns of the world." Look at it this way. The world instructs us to be in darkness. The Bible notes that sin lives in darkness. First John 1:5 says, "God is light, pure light; there's not a trace of darkness in him."[58] If we live in darkness, then we are living the way the world wants us to live, not God. First Thessalonians 5:5-8 says,

> For you are all children of the light and of the day; we don't belong to darkness and night. So be on your guard, not asleep like the others. Stay alert and be sober. Night is the time for sleep and the time when people get drunk. But let us who live in the light think clearly, protected by the body armor of faith and love, and wearing as our helmet the confidence of our salvation.[59]

Transforming and renewing your mind means to decide daily to be the light of the world and the salt of the earth. These verses give us all a visual picture of how we should live our lives. As salt and light, we are called to keep others from going bad and shine a light so that they can see.

YOUR AMBASSADORSHIP

Every civilized country of the world sends ambassadors to live in various foreign countries and represent their homeland. In 2 Corinthians 5:20, we are called Christ's ambassador, "as though God were making his appeal through us." As an ambassador of Christ, you are being called to live your life worthy of the gospel of Jesus (Philippians 1:27). As hard as it might be at times, you must never forget Who you represent.

As I've shared, I was blessed to come from a strong Christian home with parents who loved God and taught me to follow Him. I am the youngest of three and my parents' only son. I can remember from the time I was fifteen until graduation, every weekend as I would leave the house to go out with friends or on a date, my mom would say this phrase: "Don't forget who you are or whose you are." Now, as a typical teenager seeking independence, I recall getting tired of that saying. Every time, who and whose, who and whose ...but subconsciously, I think those wise words kept me from getting into trouble.

It was not until I got to college that I really took the time to think about what she was actually saying. My mother, in all her wisdom, was reminding me that I belonged to a great family and to God. Let me explain. I grew up in Montgomery, Alabama. It's not a small town, but at times it felt like one. By the time I came along into my teenage years, my family was made up of established members of the community. They were active in a large church and in various social groups, which meant more adults knew me than I knew them. My father was a very admirable and respected attorney in the city, and so I believe my mom was reminding me of the heritage that I came from. Also, she was reminding me that I belonged to God. In her own humble way, she did not want me to ever forget that I was that light on the hill. And before I went out and tried to cover that light with a shade, I needed to remember who and whose I was.

Throughout your life, you will represent many things. For instance, I represent my family. I also represent this book, my ministry, and I represent a leader in my church and community. You represent your school, family, and group of friends. In college you might represent a social group (like a Greek organization or club), maybe a ministry, and your school. Before you become a representative of various groups in college, it will be important to remember that your first allegiance is to your ambassadorship in Christ.

John is a pastor and is very well known in his community. He tells a story of taking his three young sons shopping one day at Walmart. As they were heading back to the car, John was approached by a man whom he did not recognize. The man explained that he knew John was a local pastor and had, therefore, followed him around the store, watching him interact with his kids to see if he was the "real deal." The man decided that John was real about his witness and had stopped to tell him so. Once it is known that you are a Christian and are serious about your faith, people will be watching you. Some people will be watching you to see if you are for real, and others will be watching in the hope that you will fail, so they can feel better about themselves. I think that both are reasons to make sure that you do not cause someone to stumble.

Before you join an organization on campus or get too involved with an individual or group, you need to stop and ask yourself the following questions as you try to protect your witness:

1. Can I be involved with this and still be a city on a hilltop?

2. Will this individual or group make me cover my light?

3. Can I represent Jesus and this commitment too?

4. Does this individual or group represent the same things that I represent?

The answer to these questions will be very important as you decide what you will represent in college.

FIGHTING AGAINST TEMPTATION

I hear lots of college students say that they are most tempted when they are out at parties or on dates. This is understandable because you are going to be tempted. James 4:7 says, "Resist the devil and he will flee from you."[60] I know that this is much easier said than done, but removing the temptation from your sight is a great first step. If you have a group of like-minded Christians that you spend all of your time with and you do not have other opportunities to go to parties, formals, dates, etc., then this might not be an issue, but I think for most people, it is. Let me tell you something that I learned years ago in a seminary class. I was in a class about the spiritual disciplines. We had been studying fasting.[61] Fasting is a scriptural discipline designed for you to focus on Christ while not eating; when you feel a hunger pain, you are to pray and focus on God. This was the first time I had ever fasted, and I decided to do it for three days.

The first day was hard, but I had gone a day without eating before. The second day was much harder. I recall watching TV the night of the second day, and during a commercial I saw a fifteen-inch (the size of my TV screen) cheeseburger, juicy and still smoking from the grill. In a move of desperation, I quickly changed the station and found a commercial for a huge steak dinner. Changing the channel again (I only had three

126

stations at the time), I was faced with another food commercial, so I turned the TV off. Immediately praying that the images I had just seen would vanish from my thoughts, I heard God say, "Dude, this is how you should react to sinful temptation!" This served as a vivid example of James 4:7 about resisting the devil. If not going to a party is spiritually the right decision, then that is what you should do. But I also believe it is important to your faith and to your witness that you do not close yourself off from the non-Christian world around you. Remember, Jesus went to parties and weddings and had dinner with social and moral outcasts on a regular basis. You can go out with your standards in tow, have a fun time, and feel good about yourself the next day. I believe it is a part of your witness to let others know by your actions that the abundant life in John 10:10 is a freedom to live life without fear.

THERE'S FREEDOM IN THE WORD "NO"

Many people have a hard time saying "no." They don't want to hurt someone's feelings or make someone feel disliked. In college, the word "no" can save you from a lot of hard times and problems. If you feel pressured into doing something that you think is wrong, say no! If you think some of your friends will not like you if you turn them down to go out, then maybe they aren't the type of friends that you need to have. Making alternative plans so that you are not put in that situation is a good idea so that you have an obvious reason to say no.

CAN I GET A WITNESS?

Now that we understand that we are to represent Jesus and protect our witness for Him in our lives, I would like for us to look at some specific situations that you might find yourself in while at college. From the first day you set foot on your college campus, you begin a new stage of life. In college, the organizations that you join become the groups of people that you hang out with, and therefore, that becomes the identity that you are known by. We have spent a lot of time in this section talking about decision making, using wisdom in those decisions and making sure that the choices you make reflect who you are in Christ. It is very important to your witness that your identity in Christ and your campus identity (in the eyes of those who know you well and those who don't) reflect the same things. For the remaining pages of this chapter, we will look at various options of involvement in college and what you might need to consider in an effort to be true to yourself and your faith in Christ.

GETTING INVOLVED WITH A LOCAL CHURCH AND A CHRISTIAN ORGANIZATION

As I've mentioned, most Christian college freshmen drift away from growth in their faith because they don't make wise decisions about their involvement and relationships. Most of the college freshmen that I know move off to school, possibly join a Greek organization (sometimes even before classes start), make friends with anyone and everyone, join other clubs and groups that look like fun, and then, maybe sometime later in their college career, begin to visit churches and other Christian organizations. I believe that a wise person might consider doing this at the start of college instead.

A recent survey showed that one of the biggest changes for Christian college students is the decline in church attendance. The percent of freshman in 2000 who attended church was 52 percent. Two years later, as juniors, the number had dropped to only 29 percent.[62] All colleges will have an outlet for you to be a part of fellowship, worship, and discipleship. I think you should look them over and find the one that fits you and your needs. If you go to a small college, your choices might be limited to only one or two major Christian groups. It is also important that you are active in a local church. Most college towns have great churches that are geared toward college students.

The important thing is that you find a group of believers that you can grow together with and be accountable to. Most church denominations will have an organization on campus with similar traditions of that related church. There will also be many nondenominational organizations like Cru (formerly Campus Crusade for Christ),[63] Young Life66 leadership,[64] Campus Outreach,[65] Fellowship of Christian Athletes (FCA),[66] as well as many other smaller, and equally worthy groups that you can be a valuable part of.

Before moving overseas to a mission field in Asia, a friend of mine named Matt started a great organization on a major US college campus. It was called Grace Campus Ministries. During the years of its existence, hundreds of college students gathered weekly for worship and small group discussions. In Matt's own words,

Grace Campus began out of a burden and vision for a new collegiate ministry on Auburn's campus. Specifically, our aim with students is to encourage them to understand who they are in Christ and live for the glory of His name. [College is an] exciting time ...and it can also be a lonely time for some. Either way, every student goes off to college wanting to belong to something or someone bigger than themselves. We pray they'd immerse themselves in Christian community and discover the love and grace of God in tangible ways. Hands down, Christian community is the way for students to acclimate to life as a Christian in college. From that foundation, they can be encouraged and equipped to live missional lives on their campus.

This type of organization exists on most college campuses in the United States. Finding the one that fits you the best is an important step in your continued journey of your faith.

The best way to find a church that is right for you is to start by finding a friend that has a similar church background as you. Discuss the type of church you are looking for. What kind of worship style appeals to you? Are you interested in a church with a strong college group associated with it? Do you prefer a large church with many opportunities or something small with a family-like atmosphere? Start looking by finding a listing from a campus ministry or in the student activities office. The next step is to begin visiting churches. Don't take too long though. I have known college students to spend all four years "looking" for a church, and they never get plugged in to anything. One reason some college students never find the "perfect church" is because they are looking for a church exactly like the one they grew up in. Don't try to replace your home church, but look for something that meets your needs while you are away at college. Take the search seriously, find something that fits your needs, and get involved. Your spiritual growth depends on it.

What if you could sit at the table on Thanksgiving with your family and tell them that you have found a church at college? Does that sound like a good goal to have? If so, be sure to follow the steps on page X of this book and find a new church before you go home for your first Thanksgiving as a college student.

JOINING A GREEK ORGANIZATION

The Greek system is not for everyone. I am the first to say that even though I was in a fraternity. Most fraternities and sororities will be filled with non-Christians who want to live in darkness and thrive on this lifestyle. This means that they will not only have different social objectives than you, but their entire mindset and goals will be focused on themselves and their own satisfaction. However, I joined a fraternity and have never regretted it. Sure, there were times when I was lonely because I felt like the only one who cared about his faith, but I think in a lot of ways, that prepared me for real life. As a member of a fraternity, I was part of a group of guys who truly cared about each other. I saw this as an opportunity to be salt and light, and as I got close to my brothers, I had many memorable conversations about faith and God. But it is not for everyone. If you don't feel led to do it, don't. If deep down you are afraid that it will prevent you from growing in your faith, don't join. Matthew 5:13 continues to say, "But what good is salt if it has lost its flavor?"[67]

If you are not sure what it would be like and would like to investigate it, I would say give rush a try. Most importantly, pray and God will lead you through it. But before you go through rush, think about who you are and why you want to go Greek. Are you the type of person who meets people easily? Are you someone who always needs to have people around you? Are you easily influenced to go along with the crowd? Are you comfortable to be a minority when it comes to growing in your faith? How are you with social rejection? Many Christians go into college without asking these questions. They get excited about the idea of being in a fraternity and sorority but never think through whether or not they are a good fit for one until they join and later feel stuck in it. I'm not saying that Christians can't be involved in the Greek system. As a matter of fact, I believe that the Greek system needs Christians to be involved in it. This book is about owning your faith. As an adult, you will have to live in a non-Christian society and stand strong for who you are in Christ. But if you are not to that level of faith ownership yet, you should not add fuel to the fire by joining a group that will daily test your commitment to Jesus.

One of the main reasons I think that fraternities and sororities are overwhelmingly spiritually challenging is due to a lack of leadership. A Greek organization is the only group that you may ever be a part of that essentially has no leader. At this point in your life, you have always had older leaders who could mentor you along the way. In high school you had teachers and coaches, at church you had pastors and teachers, and at home you had parents and relatives. Even in other college campus groups, there will be adults who are in charge and able to lead. In the Greek system, this is not usually the case. It is true that every chapter has a president and an executive counsel, but those roles are made up of peers who are potentially as spiritually needy as everyone else. All Greek chapters should also have adult advisors or sponsors, but those individuals are usually not involved in the day-to-day operations and leadership of the group. Again, this does not mean that you shouldn't be involved in such a group. If you can be a person who can spiritually lead, then you might be just what that organization needs, but it is important to understand what it is that you are getting involved in before you allow it to become a part of who you are in college.

For those who feel they are spiritually ready, there are many good qualities of Greek life. It is a great place to make friends and meet many types of people; plus, it's a résumé booster when you are looking for a job to say that you were a part of a nationally recognized organization. Just pay close attention to what you are joining and why you are joining it. Be sure you make the choice that will help you grow and mature in your faith and not one that will prevent your growth.

DATING

Dating in college is different than dating in high school. There are many more events to take a date to in college. Also, as you get older, dating becomes a very important part of your life. Even if you do not have a steady girlfriend/boyfriend, you have the opportunity to go out and hang out with more people of the opposite sex. It is statistically true that many people meet their spouse while in college. Dating is one of the most important issues in which you will have to use wisdom and make good decisions. It is truly better not to date at all than to find the wrong person to get involved with. You will have to be very careful and know your limits before you get into a situation that you can't easily get out of. I have personally known many Christians who have started a dating relationship without including God in the mix, and they now regret their decisions. They met, found what they thought was love, and began exploring sex, all within the first six months of their relationship. Sex is the beginning of the end of a dating relationship. In a counseling setting, I can always tell when a dating couple has had sex, even without them ever telling me.

When your relationship focus moves to the physical, you will begin to see problems with the emotional, relational, and spiritual aspects of the relationship. Sex only lasts within a marriage, and if you will think of that person as someone's future wife or future husband, it should put it all in perspective. You may think that things are getting serious and that this person might be your future spouse, but that will not be official until you say "I do." The only way to cultivate a healthy, Christ-focused dating relationship is to submerge it in prayer. If a couple will pray together regularly and make Christ the center of the relationship, if it is meant to be, a pure love will soon evolve. If not, know that God will have someone else waiting for you down the road.

I want to talk to the guys for a moment about dating. You know, guys, we are different from girls when it comes to sex and dating. For us, it is a very physical thing, but to them it is very emotional. Guys, as a whole, have gotten very good at manipulating the emotional strings of girls to get what we want. Even many Christian guys know what to say and when to say it to get girls to do things that are not healthy spiritually or relationally. To the guys I want to say, "Be the man!" The Bible is clear about the husband leading the wife spiritually. So look at this as a practice run. The girl you are dating, or will date, may or may not become your wife, but the chances are good that she will become someone's wife. Be the man in your relationship. Lead her in purity and respect, and if you love her, show her by what you don't tempt her to do with you. Sex is a great thing when you are married. God created it to be pure and holy. It is true that all the times the Bible mentions sex, it never talks about sex being a bad or dirty thing. The only negative slant the Bible takes on sex is when it is not used in a pure and holy way (Romans 13:13, 1 Corinthians 6:13, Ephesians 5:3).

If I may, let me now speak to the females for a moment. Ladies, since I am not one of you, I cannot relate to you in this way. But I can ask that you look for a guy who is serious about his faith and about honoring you. You are worth it! I wish I could express to you what my wife means to me. She really is my partner in life; she is the best mother that I have ever seen; and she is one of the wisest people I have ever met. Before she and I started dating during my senior year in college (her freshmen year), I had a number of girlfriends that I thought were "the one." I spent years trying to fit a circle into a square hole relationally, but none of them worked. Once I met my wife, I knew that she was it. Since that day I have tried to love, honor, and respect her the best way I know how. Don't waste your time with a guy who's anything less than someone who will love and cherish you. If he is not ready to lead you closer to Jesus, then he is not ready for you! God made you to be holy—Ephesians 1:4.

DEALING WITH BIASED, ANTI-CHRISTIAN COLLEGE PROFESSORS

In general, much of the college academic community in this county is a liberal, nonreligious group that seeks to teach its views unfairly to students who often are too intimidated to speak up. You will likely be faced with professors teaching evolution as the only possible explanation of the world's formation and ideas of moral relativity, which state that determining right from wrong depends solely on an individual's own ideals and cultural viewpoint rather than on the Word of God. Many classes will criticize the Bible and debate its authenticity as well as the very existence of God. According to Focus on the Family, over 25 percent of college professors in the United States are agnostic or atheist. If you go to what they call "elite schools," that number jumps to over 40 percent. In the fields of biology and psychology, it is as high as 60 percent. The study also notes that over 50 percent of college professors regard the Bible as fable or legend rather than the true Word of God.[68] As a Christian, you must be alert not to believe every perspective that you are taught in class.

Professors are well aware of the influence they have over young students, and if you are new to your faith (or even if you are not), it is hard to stand up to a professor's atheist philosophy. You must be ready to defend yourself and know what you believe and why you believe it. God will lead you in situations like this. This professor is on his/her own, full of ideas and speculations. You have the Creator of the world on your side with truth and wisdom.

It is so important at this stage of your life to know, not only what you believe, but to know why you believe it. Most Christians know what they believe. They can tell you that they believe Jesus died on the cross to save the world from sin and that if you commit your life to Christ, you will live in eternity with Him in heaven. Most Christians will agree that the Bible is the Word of God and that it is God breathed (2 Timothy 3:16). But how do you know? If you answer "faith" or "because that's what I was taught," then I would say that your reasoning is not any different than people of other faiths. Yet, if Jesus said that He is the way, truth, and life and no one gets to God without going through Him, then those other faiths are misguided. How do you know that what you believe is right? If you say that you don't know, then I would say that the agnostic professor will know how to confuse and cause you to doubt. To many professors, blind faith is a joke. An agnostic lives his life on proof that there is no God, but we, as Christians, live our life not needing physical proof that there is a God. Josh McDowell, in his book Don't Check Your Brains at the Door says,

Jesus told His followers, "You will know the truth, and the truth will set you free" (John 8:32) ... Jesus does not call upon us to commit intellectual suicide in trusting Him as Savior and Lord. He does not expect us to exercise our Christian faith in an intellectual vacuum. The Christian's faith must be a faith based on evidence.[69]

The proof that Jesus was and did what the Bible says He did is found in the testimonies of those who were there. Any courtroom today will base evidence on eyewitnesses. The only proof we have that George Washington lived and was the first president of the United States is the testimonies of those who lived with him (a fact probably not contested by any professor). We don't know that the picture on the one-dollar bill is really George Washington unless the person who drew it said that it was indeed Washington. We couldn't say for sure that he was a great general and president unless thousands of people had attested to his existence.

John wrote in John 20:30-31, "Jesus did many other miraculous signs in the presence of his disciples, which are not recorded in this book. But these are written that you may believe that Jesus is the Christ, the Son of God, and that by believing you may have life in his name."[70] John wrote this because he saw it with his very eyes. Yes, he could have been lying! All of the disciples could have been lying when they spent the rest of their lives preaching this Word and dying for it. It is true that people have died for a lie. But no one has died for a lie that they didn't think was truth. These twelve men spent every day with Jesus for three years. They saw the miracles and watched Jesus die. They then saw Him alive and spent forty more days with a Jesus with holes in His hands and feet. If this was a lie, these men knew it, and they gave the rest of their lives for that lie. The proof in Jesus is in the testimonies of the people who knew Jesus personally. This is unfaultable evidence.

DRINKING ALCOHOL

Let's talk about drinking for a moment. Alcohol is the number one social issue among college students, and it is everywhere in college. It will be at parties, on your dorm hall, snuck into sporting events, and offered to you on many occasions during your time in school. The first issue about drinking is if you are under age, it is against the law for you to drink. Though I am aware that this is not a deterrent to most students, it is dangerous, can tarnish your witness, and can get you in a lot of trouble. Take it from me—it's not as fun as it looks!

But what about when you do become of legal age to drink alcohol? What does the Bible say about that? If you are of age to drink, there is nothing in Scripture that says you can't drink alcohol as long as you don't drink so much that your mind is distracted from focusing on God (Ephesians 5:18). But what if you are twenty-one years old, you are drinking responsibly, and someone sees you who is young in their faith and/or is struggling with alcohol? Or what if someone sees you who strongly believes that any drinking is wrong? What do you say? Do you say, "That is their problem; I'm not doing anything wrong"? Many Christians do!

Something that we must consider is that drinking is very taboo in this country. The fact that it is so intolerable to some people means that we must be that much more careful about dealing with it. Romans 14:13 says, "Live in such a way that you will not cause another believer to stumble and fall."[71] You see, in Paul's day, the question came up about whether or not meat sacrificed to idols could be eaten. To those Christians who had worshiped idols prior to knowing Christ, this was a very serious issue. To them, eating that meat was the equivalent of worshiping those idols. But to other Christians, the meat was simply food with no spiritual significance. This, a very taboo situation of that day, caused an uproar in Rome. Paul, setting everyone straight, said that technically there is nothing wrong with eating the meat, but if it caused someone to struggle in his faith, then you should not do it. He says in verses 20-22:

Don't tear apart the work of God over what you eat. Remember, there is nothing wrong with these things in themselves. But it is wrong to eat anything if it makes another person stumble. Don't eat meat or drink wine or do anything else if it might cause another Christian to stumble. You may have the faith to believe that there is nothing wrong with what you are doing, but keep it between yourself and God.[72]

This is an interesting passage because it affirms that Christians are at different places in their faith, and we, as the body of Christ, are all responsible for each other's growth. First Corinthians 8:9, 12 says, "Be careful, however, that the exercise of your freedom does not become a stumbling block to the weak. When you sin against your brother in this way and wound their weak conscience, you sin against Christ."[73] Then verse 13 goes on to say that it is better not to drink or whatever else you think might cause your brother to stumble, so that you do not chance it. First Corinthians 14:23 concludes by saying, "If you do anything you believe is not right, you are sinning."[74]

The most important thing to remember when you are out in the world is that you are a child of God, Christ's ambassador, the light of the world. You must be alert to always protect your witness. Remember who you are and whose you are when you are out at a party or alone with a date. You are a witness for Christ, and your faith and the faith of others (and even the future faith of nonbelievers) will be affected one way or another by what you say and by the way you live your life.

TRANSCEND

SECTION THREE

Chapter Seven
GIVING YOUR LIFE AWAY

Natalie went to church a few times as a child. Her parents weren't very serious about God, so naturally Natalie was not either. In high school she was very popular. She loved to party and was drunk and stoned most every weekend. One spring break, just after Natalie broke up with her boyfriend, she and some friends rented a condo on the beach. It was there that Natalie became so depressed that she decided to kill herself. Natalie decided that she would wait until everyone was asleep, then take enough sleeping pills so that she would never wake up. Natalie was ready to end her life, except that Elizabeth, a friend of Natalie's, sensed something was wrong and would not leave her alone. Every time Natalie would wake up during the night, Elizabeth was there and awake. A few days later, Elizabeth asked Natalie to join her on a weekend trip with her church group. Natalie went, and that's where she met Julia. Julia was a leader on the trip, and that night in the hotel room, Natalie asked Julia about her faith. Julia told her about a God who loved her more than she could imagine. That night, only a few months before Natalie would graduate from high school, she accepted Jesus in her life.

Realizing that life would never be the same, Natalie went home and told her family and friends about the decision she had made. She got involved in the church and was discipled by Julia over the next year. After a few years of growing in her faith, Natalie got involved in a ministry and started developing mentoring friendships with teenage girls who were going through the same things that she had once gone through. Looking back, Natalie knows that God was protecting her all along and preparing her for a life with a purpose.

The greatest joy that you can have in your faith is to give your life away. What do I mean by this? Let me share with you part three of my college story. After the summer trip to Russia, I knew that my life had changed forever. I returned home from that trip with a fresh outlook on my life and a brand new perspective of my future, which I had no idea was about to change forever. You see, when I was a senior in high school, I felt like God wanted me to be in ministry one day. I pocketed that information and pulled it back out in Russia. By the time I returned, I knew I was being called into full-time ministry to teenagers. Even before I got home, I knew that I had some changes to make in my life. I had been in a two-year dating relationship that I felt had to end. We got along pretty well but had two very different ideas of our life together. I felt that the best thing for me to do at that time was to end the relationship. The fall of that year I moved back to school for my senior year. It was not going to be a very difficult year academically, and I was excited to experience it. I was a Young Life leader at a local high school and served as the administrative vice president of the Student Government Association. I was tired of fraternity life by this point, and so I moved off campus to actively become a recluse. My prayer was that I was finished with dating until God was ready for me to meet my wife. I was actually honest about this and was not trying to trick God into introducing me to my wife sooner than He had planned. So I got serious about my faith (regained ownership of it), began to make plans about ministry and seminary, and hung my hat up on dating. Life was good! But about two months into my new spiritual voyage, in a comedic act by the Lord Almighty, I met this cute blonde freshman named Andrea that I would eventually fall head over heels for, date for three years, and marry. The story is great, if you have a minute ...

As I said, it was my senior year. I was tired of playing frat boy and was ready to graduate and move on in life (in the same way that every high school senior is ready to graduate the day they begin the twelfth grade). One Friday night— October 22, 1993, to be exact—I went over to the fraternity hall because I was bored. I had not been up there much that fall and had not met any of the new freshman girls, a rarity for me in Octobers past. So I was sitting in the chapter room talking to

149

Chris, a fellow senior fraternity brother. Andrea was there because she had asked Chris to her pledge formal the next night and was trying to get to know him before the date. Chris and I were talking about life and the things most important to us in life. After Chris shared, I turned to the cute girl next to me that I still had not yet officially met and asked, "What do you want most out of life?" to which she replied that she just wanted to be a "godly wife and mother." Well (girls, take note), my heart melted. We ended up talking more that night. Then about seven of us made a late night run to Waffle House where I remember having more fun talking to this girl who seemed to be different from any other girl I had ever met before.

The next night, while Andrea was at the pledge formal with Chris, I went to the movies with my fraternity little brother Brandon, who was a stud but oddly enough (and I've never thought about this until now as I write) was not invited to the sorority pledge formal. I asked him on the way to the movie who he planned to take to our upcoming Halloween party. He boasted about having a few girls in mind, and when he said that Andrea was at the top of his list, I made a quick decision. After hearing the name that had caused me to ask in the first place, I immediately pulled rank on my "little brother" and told him to pick another because I was going to ask Andrea that next day. That Sunday, I found out from my sources that she was watching intramural soccer (which really meant hanging out with friends on the intramural soccer fields). I remember pulling up on my bike like Lancelot on his steed and asking her to the party, which was the next weekend. We ended up spending almost every day together that week and had a great time at the party. We dated until she graduated, got married in 1996, and moved to Texas to go on staff with Young Life to change the world.

I tell you all of this to say that dating life in college can have a happy ending. I began college as a kid, searching for purpose and acceptance outside the Christian bubble in which I grew up in. I struggled spiritually for a few years before growing up enough to realize that my ancient paths were leading to the good way, which is what I truly desired. I began to transform my faith the year before I went to Russia, where God showed me that He had never left me but had carried me for most of the way. My senior year in college was all about learning and understanding purpose and calling. There is no way for you to get to your purpose before you first transform. But once you discover purpose, you learn about a calling that has awaited you all along.

DEVELOPING INTO THE PERSON YOU WERE MADE TO BE

What is the best gift you have ever gotten? Was it a bike for Christmas, or maybe a car for your sixteenth birthday? The best Christmas gift I ever got was a guitar when I was seventeen. I had borrowed a guitar for about two years after I learned to play, but I knew I wanted one of my own. So for Christmas I got a brand new black Washburn D12 acoustic guitar with a Martin thin line pickup. I was pumped! It was the one—I had picked it out of a music magazine and had hoped that my parents had taken the hints. It was a Washburn because they were cool; it had a pickup because a buddy and I were starting a band; and it was black because it was 1989 and Bono played a black acoustic in the "With or Without You"[75] video (why else?). It was a great guitar, and I still play it often.

Gifts are fun to give and fun to receive. But to ask about your favorite gift is a trick question because we have been given many gifts that we do not even know about yet. The Bible is very clear that all Christians are equipped with many spiritual gifts to do God's work. Here is how it works. God designed us to live for a certain purpose. He knew what our life was going to be like even before we were born. So when He made us, He planted certain gifts in us only to be fostered once we begin a relationship with Him. Many of these gifts may be unseen at this point in your life. For example, if you had told me as a teenager that I would grow up to love writing, I would have laughed. Better yet, if you could have told my high school English teachers that I would one day be a writer, they would have sent you to the office. I did not learn to love writing until I got out of school and started writing for fun rather than for an assignment. But this gift is in me and has been growing in me since I was born. My mom saw it years before anyone else did. She would always tell me in high school and college that I expressed myself well in writing. Then, it might have only been a birthday card or thank you note, but she saw the gift. In high school I started writing music and found that lyric writing came easy for me. Over time, I felt like I was being drawn to writing even though I did not know what that meant. For example, the summer after I graduated from college I served as the summer youth guy for a small church and found myself wanting to write Bible studies. I remember thinking, I don't write! What am I doing? But God was nourishing that seed He had planted in me at birth. God knew I would write this book and that you would one day read it. Often I wonder what He was doing with this gift when I needed it to pass tenth grade English. But it was there waiting on me to use for His purpose. Now, I write books, articles, curriculums and Bible studies, blog posts, tweets, status updates, and still the occasional note with a real pen and paper.

As you think about your future in regard to your calling, let me tell you not to worry about if you will be able to handle it or not. God will never put something in your life that you cannot handle. With every opportunity, He will give you the gifts to do the work. Paul writes in 1 Corinthians, "Now there are different kinds of gifts, but it is the same Holy Spirit who is the source of them all. A spiritual gift is given to each of us as a means of helping the entire church."[76]

WHAT IS YOUR MINISTRY?

If I were to ask you if you were in full-time ministry, what would you say? Most would say "no." But what if I told you that I believe every Christian is designed for full-time ministry? I'm not talking about a ministry job like a pastor or a missionary, but rather a full-time pursuit of ministry to others. I define ministry as a lifelong quest of representing Christ and working to lead others to Him. This can be done as you live your life and interact with society. Basically, it is living your life for Christ and being His ambassador in the world, leading others to Him with your actions and words. So I ask again, are you in full-time ministry?

I believe that everyone was made for a reason, a purpose to be used for the glory of God. The journey of life is about finding out what that purpose is and then spending the rest of your life doing a job well done. Sadly, many people never discover their purpose because they are too busy to hear God. So many Christians are content with going to church and living a moral life but never find the joy of giving their life away to other people in ministry. The fact is God doesn't need you to spread His truth, but He wants you to be a part of what He is doing. When Jesus calls people to follow Him, He says don't just follow me, do what I am doing: love people, help people, and tell people of the hope found in Christ.

Ministry is not only for those who have a full-time job at a church or those called to be missionaries. Everyone is gifted enough to be in ministry. It is true that for some, life's purpose is to be a great evangelist and lead thousands to Jesus. For others, it is to be the parents who raises their child to be a doctor who saves lives in the name of Jesus. Some people are called to a secular job that earns enough income to allow them to support those on the front lines of ministry. Many people's purpose is to get a job in the cubical next to someone who is hurting and be a light in the office place. A few people are put into the public spotlight to shine Christ to the masses. Others will be the neighbor who sees it as her calling to minister to those hurting most in the community. God has a purpose for everyone, even you!

So what do you think it will be for you? What are you good at? What are you passionate about? There is no doubt that God has already begun to prepare you for great things. He has and will continue to put people and opportunities in your life to prepare you for a life of purpose. Paul writes, "I am sure that God, who began the good work within you, will continue His work until it is finally finished on that day when Jesus Christ comes back again."[77] A great thing about God's providence is that even before He reveals a ministry opportunity to us, He is working hard to prepare us for it.

My friend Donnie has been in ministry for over twenty-five years, though he has never received a paycheck for it. Donnie was a volunteer leader for Young Life where he made a difference in the lives of countless people, including me. In case you are not familiar with the role of a Young Life leader, his main responsibility is to build friendships and relationships with high school guys. It can be a hard job trying to spend enough time with a high school guy to develop that relationship. The other thing you should know about Donnie is that he is the biggest Alabama Crimson Tide fan I have ever known. This guy goes to every football game and most of the baseball and basketball games. He has even been known to catch a gymnastic or swim meet throughout the year. Anyway, so by the time

Donnie was a senior in high school, he had grown a lot in his faith because of the relationship he had with his Young Life leader. With plans to go to the University of Alabama since birth, there was no question that Donnie was ready for college. His senior year, his Young Life leader asked him a question that would change his life, my life, and the lives of who knows how many teenagers over the next couple of decades. Donnie was asked to consider staying in his hometown, going to a small local college, and joining the Young Life staff in a part-time college student staff role. This would mean giving up a life-long dream to go to the University of Alabama, but because of God's call, Donnie took this offer, stayed all four years in his hometown and then spent the next quarter of a century as a volunteer Young Life leader, giving eight to ten hours a week to ministry with teenagers. God gave Donnie a job that allows him to earn a good living and have enough time to fulfill his calling as a Young Life leader as well.

As we have discovered in Romans 12:2, God gives us His two-step plan of finding our life purpose and calling. He instructs us that if we will focus on Him by not conforming to the world but transforming our minds, we will know His will for our lives. That's when Ephesians 4:1 takes it one step further by saying, "I ...beg you to lead a life worthy of your calling, for you have been called by God."[78] This verse challenges us to not only find out what

157

our calling is, but to do it 110 percent. To live your life worthy of your calling means to dedicate yourself to the Lord—to be faithful and willing to serve. And as I've said, for most people this life of service will not be in the spotlight or in a paid ministry job, but rather will be a life of ministry, giving to others what has been given to you. Even though all of us have a different purpose in life and are equipped with different gifts, our first calling is to live as the light of the world—to be Christ's ambassador and to show a conforming world that we are different. And believe me, they notice.

The week before I graduated from college, my fraternity had an alumni ceremony for the brothers who were graduating. During the ceremony, those of us who were becoming alumni sat in front and had an opportunity to say a few words to the rest of the group. It was full of "remember when ..." and "I'll never forget ..." I don't really remember what I said that night, but I do remember what happened next.

After we got a chance to speak, the rest of the fraternity got the opportunity to address us. I was expecting my brothers to give me a friendly sendoff, but I was shocked to hear guy after guy say to me that I was the only person they knew who stood for something. I had friends that I had debated about God with say that they knew there was a God because of the way I lived my life. I was so shocked that I could barely breathe. I have already told you that I felt I had spent two and a half years of college spiritually stagnant. In my opinion, I had let God down by not being a spiritual role model for my fellow frat brothers. But that is not how they saw it. To them, I was a disciple. They learned about God from me.

I still get chills thinking about it because I didn't do anything to deserve those words of praise. God moved within me, and I did not even know it. Before I even knew what an ancient path was, God used me. Before I ever stepped foot on a college campus, God began a good work in me that would change the lives of people I did not even know yet. I had a calling to be a light to the guys in my fraternity, and even though I fought that calling at times, God still used me to an effective end. Even today I am surprised at how God chooses to use me. I have been working with teenagers for over a decade and giving them wisdom that I didn't know I had. I say and do things that I know I am not wise enough to come up with by myself. I'm a dyslexic, life-long poor student who was told by high school guidance counselors and college professors that I would never make it at the next level …and now I'm writing books? God can use you! God will use you! He is already using you! He has begun a work in you that will continue past college and forever. Why? Because He loves you and because you care enough about Him to transform your life and be that light on your campus and in the world.

While you are in college, you will find many opportunities to be involved in a ministry where you can give your life away to others. Most of the organizations that I mentioned in chapter six are looking for people to join. They will need people to help promote worship and discipleship events as well as lead those events. Are you good at making things like signs and posters? Do you play an instrument or sing? You might find a niche there. Do you feel led to start a small group Bible study with your friends? Could you lead it, or do you know someone who could? If so, I would suggest a guys or girls only group because people are more open when the sexes are separated. Find a book in the Bible to read together or a Christian growth book to read and discuss. How about short-term mission trips? Lots of these organizations take summer mission trips to other places where they build churches, lead Bible schools or sports clinics, and share the gospel with people who do not know Him. Remember my story about my trip to Russia? It literally changed my life. These are all opportunities where you can make a difference through your ministry.

I would like to share one more ministry outlet that I believe is one of the most amazing opportunities you could ever have. Young Life is a relationship-based outreach ministry to junior high and high school students. Its mission is to lead kids to Christ and help them grow in their faith. A Young

Life leader is someone who is committed to Christ and has a heart for lost kids. Many college campuses have a Young Life leader training program. During this time, you learn what it means to follow Christ, and you are trained to build friendships with younger teenagers. Once you become a YL leader, you are put on a team with other leaders and go to the school and hang out with kids: building a friendship, then a relationship, and over time, changing their life in Christ.

I was a Young Life kid in high school. I grew up in church, but it was not until I got to know my Young Life leader that I really understood what having a relationship with Jesus was all about. My junior year in college, I became a Young Life leader. It was at that time that I started to take ownership of my faith, just prior to the trip to Russia. After two years as a volunteer YL leader, I knew what God wanted me to do with my life. After graduation I spent two years as a youth pastor while in seminary and then went on staff with Young Life. I served on staff with Young Life for fifteen years, only resigning from that ministry to start TheTransMission in 2010.

I will be the first to say that Young Life leadership is not for everyone. It requires more of a commitment than some of the other opportunities that I mentioned before. Mostly, I hope you will see that there are lots of chances for you to get involved with a ministry, to grow, and to help others grow in the journey with Jesus.

CREATING A PERSONAL MISSION STATEMENT

If you owned a business or were CEO of a major corporation, you would have a mission statement. This statement would show your clients and customers who you are by telling them what you believe about yourself and your product. Chick-fil-A, one of my favorite restaurants, has a bold mission statement that clearly represents the founder, Truett Cathy, and his commitment to Christ: "To glorify God by being a faithful steward of all that is entrusted to us and to have a positive influence on all who come in contact with Chick-fil-A."[79] Krispy Kreme, another preferred eating establishment of mine, posts their mission statement right on the side of the box of doughnuts: "We promise to continue to make good-tasting, high-quality products because that's what you expect and deserve, and that's what we expect of ourselves."[80] Each of these companies takes their service seriously. They have this commitment to us, the consumer, and to themselves. As an avid supporter of both Krispy Kreme and Chick-fil-A, I can say without a doubt that both fulfill this pledge.

What about you and me? We too have pledged to serve. If we are serious about our faith, then we must be serious about being a light in the world. A personal mission statement is a great way to commit yourself to your mission and purpose. A few years ago, I developed my own mission statement to reflect my desire to serve God and be His ambassador. My personal mission statement is made up of three verses that are important to me and consequently are all shared in this book. My personal mission statement is as follows: "I will always do Romans 12:2 so that I can live out Ephesians 4:1 to experience John 10:10b." Basically what I am saying in this statement is that I will stop conforming to the world and continue to transform and renew my mind in order to know my life's purpose, so I can live my life worthy of that purpose to have an abundant, full life in Christ. Notice that my mission statement is not a commitment to do a better job in ministry, be nicer to people, or give more to the poor. Rather, it is a summarizing declaration of who I am in Christ and what I want to live for. If I take this statement seriously, I will do a better job in ministry, be nicer to people, and give to the poor. I do these things not because they are objectives on a checklist but as an overflow of my love and commitment to Jesus Christ.

I want to challenge you to think about what your mission statement might be. It does not have to be like mine, and it probably shouldn't be because it needs to come from your heart. Think about how you see yourself in the body of Christ. Who do you think God wants you to be? Think about this and write it out. Once you come up with a personal mission statement, you should have a clearer picture of who you are in Christ and how to give your life away to serve Him.

Chapter Eight
SET APART

"Where are you going?" Amy's mom asked the day after Amy returned home from school for the summer.

"Going to find a quiet place to pray and read," answered Amy on her way out the door with a Diet Coke and her backpack.

"Oh ...okay," said Amy's mother, wondering who this girl had become.

Amy was not always the type to outwardly live out her relationship with Jesus. In high school she was a pretty normal teenage girl. Her parents had not forced her to go to church, and once she graduated from high school, she went to a large university and got involved with a few Christian student organizations. She joined them at first because that's what everyone else was doing. She did not realize that a few years later her life would change forever.

After spending a year involved with the organizations, she was asked to be one of the student leaders of one of the groups. As a part of the leadership team, Amy was discipled and taught how to grow in her relationship with Jesus. She spent many opportunities serving others at camps and building relationships with those who were also growing in their faith.

Once Amy moved home for the summer before her junior year, it was natural for her to wake up, grab her Bible and journal, and find a quiet place to be alone with Jesus. As natural as it was for Amy, it was not normal for her mom who had not been there to see Amy's growth. Not only did Amy make a difference in the ministry that she was involved in at school, but she also became a living witness to her family and all of her friends at home.

Have you ever wondered what it would be like to be the president of the United States? Everyone in the world knows who you are. Every move you make is watched and protected, and every time you go somewhere, twenty police cars guide your way. In 1995, I got the opportunity to meet George W. Bush. I was living in Texas at the time, and he was my governor. I lived in a small town about an hour south of Dallas, and he was on a tour of small town courthouses. I heard he was coming, so I grabbed a friend and went down to a closed-off alleyway across the street from the county courthouse. I got there early, but I really did not need to. Only about fifty people showed up to hear him speak. To the locals, it wasn't a big deal for the governor to come speak. I, not being an official Texan, saw it as an opportunity to see the son of a former president and possibly the next president of the United States. I got there before he did, so I just walked up and stood about ten feet from his portable podium. When "W" showed up, he spoke for about ten minutes and then walked around meeting everyone. This was a few years before he began to campaign for the presidency, yet even then, I was a little shocked at the lack of security and the accessibility I had to him. I walked right up to Bush, shook his hand, and got a picture with him.

Fast forward to March of 2005. I had another chance to hear Bush speak in a gymnasium in my hometown of Montgomery, Alabama. This time, as President George W. Bush, he seemed to be a little less accessible. Once he flew in on Air Force One, all traffic on the interstate was completely stopped for about an hour while he was in route to the venue. After acquiring a ticket at the last minute, I waited in line for about two hours to finally go through a series of metal detectors and the Secret Service. Once I got in, I stood in the back of the balcony to hear him speak on social security. Once he was finished, they locked up the interstates again, drove him to his airplane, and flew him to his next stop where the Secret Service were waiting, and people were still scrambling around to find last-minute tickets.

There is a big difference in your next-door neighbor and the governor of your state. And there is a huge difference between the life of your governor and that of the president. The president of the United States is set apart from everybody else in the world. He is clearly the most significant and influential person in the world. No one, unless deemed necessary by Secret Service, gets close to the president of the United States. When he is on the road, you cannot be. When he is in the air, you cannot be. It's even against the law to publicly threaten his life. The president is set apart because of his power, influence, and authority.

Scripturally, to be set apart is to be holy. It means to be different from the world—to be Christlike. Throughout the New Testament when the attributes of a Christian are described, holiness is almost always listed. Ephesians 1:4 says, "God chose us to be holy."[81] First Thessalonians 4:7 says that "God has called us to be holy, not to live impure lives."[82] In Romans 12:1, the verse just before the appeal to stop conforming and start transforming your life, Paul writes, "I plead with you to give your bodies to God. Let them be a living and holy sacrifice, the kind He will accept. When you think of what He has done for you, is this too much to ask?"[83] In the NIV it says doing this is your "spiritual act of worship." Stop and think about that for a moment: your spiritual act of worship! Let's look at that entire passage in the NIV:

Therefore, I urge you, brothers, in the view of God's mercy, to offer your bodies as living sacrifices, holy and pleasing to God-this is your spiritual act of worship. Do not conform any longer to the patterns of this world, but be transformed by the renewing of your mind. Then you will be able to test and approve what God's will is—His good, pleasing, and perfect will.[84]

Your entire transition into the next stage of your life rests on your willingness to worship God by setting yourself apart from the world and focusing your mind and body on Christ, as you discover God's Will and purpose for your life.

YOUR SPIRITUAL ACT OF WORSHIP

For the rest of this chapter, I would like for us to look at some practical things you can do to enhance your spiritual life and grow closer in your relationship with God. These are all things that I have done in my life to grow in my faith, and I hope they will help you as well.

Your spiritual act of worship, as it says in Romans 12:1, is to be "holy and pleasing to God." The way you do this is to spend time with Him and involve Him in your life. To a new Christian, the concept of spending time with God might seem strange. You might say that you have never seen or heard God, so how can you spend time with Him?

The truth is that God seeks a relationship with us. As with any relationship, time together is the key. In my marriage, Andrea and I spend lots of time together. Our relationship has grown over the years because of that time spent and the conversations we have had. Communication is crucial to the survival of any relationship. So why would you think it would be different with your relationship with God?

THINK LIKE GOD

The way to understand how to relate to God is to know how to think like God. Now, I do not want to suggest that I know how God thinks, for that is certainly way beyond my comprehension, but one thing I have noticed throughout Scripture is that God is more concerned with our heart, our spiritual selves, than He is with the physical. Let me explain. As human beings, our first concern is always our physical situation. We want to have a good job, a nice car, and a stress-free life. Those are all physical desires. God, on the other hand, wants us to be loving, kind, considerate, and giving. Those are all matters of the heart. So when Colossians 3:2 says to set your mind on heavenly things, and Ephesians 5:1 says, "Follow God's example in everything you do, because you are His dear children. Live a life filled with love of others, following the example of Christ,"[85] we have to understand how. First Peter 4:1 says, "Since Jesus went through everything you're going through and more, learn to think like Him."[86]

This idea of thinking in spiritual terms, like God, is illustrated in the Sermon on the Mount in Matthew 5. Jesus says in verse 21, "You have heard that the law of Moses says, 'Do not murder.' If you commit murder, you are subject to judgment. But I say, if you are angry with someone, you are subject to judgment."[87] Most people would agree, murder and anger are completely different in their severity. In our everyday lives, we see angry people everywhere. I would even go so far as to say that hate, if considered justified, would not even be seen as a negative act. So why would Jesus declare that hating someone and killing them hold the same spiritual outcome? Let's look at another example. Jesus declares in verse 27, "You have heard that the law of Moses says, 'Do not commit adultery.' But I say, anyone who even looks at a woman with lust in his eyes has already committed adultery with her in his heart."[88] What? The concept of looking in lust and acting in lust being the same completely contradicts any worldly view or thought. In our mind, these are not equal, but to God they are the same because of the condition of the heart. If love, joy, peace, patience, and kindness are components of a godly life, then there is no room for hateful anger in our lives. And if goodness, faithfulness, gentleness, and self-control are the fruit of our spiritual life, just the thought of sin is enough to drive a wedge between us and God. God thinks in terms of the spiritual. If we are to understand His ways, we should learn to think this way, too.

Chances are, if you have ever spent one day in Sunday school or in vacation bible school as a kid, you are familiar with the golden rule. The golden rule comes from Christ's words in Matthew 7:12, "Do for others what you would like them to do for you. This is a summary of all that is taught in the law and the prophets."[89] Jesus gives us this command and says above all else, put others before yourself. This is a spiritual concept, not a worldly one. Putting others before yourself does not make sense in the world of business, sports, or even academics. Our natural reaction to life's situations is to want to get ahead of others. Something that I find interesting is that this idea of putting others before yourself is not unique to Christianity. Actually, the golden rule is a moral guideline that every major religion claims as its own. The Hindu religion says, "This is the sum of duty: do naught to others which if done to thee would cause thee pain."[90] In the Jewish Talmud we find, "What is hateful to you, do not to your fellow men. That is the entire Law; all the rest is commentary."[91] Buddhists believe, "Hurt not others with that which pains yourself."[92] And Islam practices, "No one of you is a believer until he desires for his brother that which he desires for himself."[93] The point is that this concept of putting others first is universal, but what I find most intriguing is how rare it is as a practice in the world.

If we are to set our minds like that of Christ, then we should try to live like He did—putting others before Himself. This takes humility. Ephesians 4:3, the verse immediately after the one that challenges us to live a life worthy of our calling says, "Be humble and gentle. Be patient with each other, making allowance for each other's faults because of your love."[94] As you attempt daily to keep your thoughts on God, you should try to practice the golden rule at all times. This is something that I try to do every day of my life, and in the process it has taught me patience and self-control. Let me give you some real examples.

Let's say that you are meeting your friends for fast food and the line is long, but luckily your friends are already in line and wanting you to cut. That's when you realize that everyone in line is as hungry as you are, and you question yourself, "How would I feel if someone cut in front of me?" Or maybe you are late for work and driving fast. A car pulls out two blocks in front of you, but because you were doing 50 mph rather than the posted 35, it makes you have to hit your breaks. When that happens, what do you do? Do you honk the horn and let them know how mad that made you? Do you ride their bumper to let them know that they have caused you to be later to work than before? Do you pass them in the left lane, yell a four-letter word, and hope that they don't see the ICHTHUS fish on back of your car? If so, ask yourself, "If I had not been speeding, would this have caused me to get mad? Would it make me angry if someone got mad at me because they were speeding?" How about this one? (If I have not already stepped on your toes, I'm probably about to.) Have you ever copied music from a friend and thought nothing about burning it rather than buying your own copy? Do you think that is fair to the artist? I know many of you reading this are thinking that it doesn't hurt anyone to do this, but musician friends of mine have felt the pinch of people burning rather than buying. What's the difference between illegally copying music and walking into a gas station and walking out with a Coke without paying for it? Other than downloading music is easier, nothing! Basically, anytime you selfishly put yourself before someone else, it's hurtful. That's why, when asked the most important commandment in Scripture, Jesus responded to love Him with all you are, then love others like you love yourself.[95]

KEEP ON PRAYING

Prayer is communication with God. I'm not talking about a "God is great, God is good," prayer before dinner, but rather time spent sharing your thoughts, ideas, issues, and frustrations with God. You might say that God already knows your thoughts, ideas, issues, and frustrations, and you are right, but just as I know that my wife loves me, to hear it every day still means a lot to me.

An active prayer life is vital to ongoing spiritual growth. Colossians 4:2 says to "devote yourselves to prayer with an alert mind and a thankful heart."[96] James 5:16 states, "the earnest prayer of a righteous person has great power and wonderful results."[97] First Thessalonians 5:17 says, "Keep on praying."[98] This verse emphasizes the importance of prayer as it stresses how often we should pray. Another translation says, "Pray continually."[99] It's not that you have to pray a certain amount of times per week or at a particular time of day; it's more about keeping God in your thoughts and including Him in every decision.

I am a very visual learner. I have always had to find tricks and methods to help me learn. Prayer was the same way for me. I have always taken 1 Thessalonians 5:17 literally, yet how can you "pray without ceasing" as the King James Version records it? During my junior year in college, I decided that I wanted to spend my day in prayer, to pray without ceasing, in an effort to renew my mind. I came up with a trick to help me focus my mind on Christ. I began setting my watch to chime every hour, so that when I heard the chime, it would remind me to stop and say a sentence prayer. So every hour I would hear the chime and thank God for the person I was currently talking to or pray for a need that was on my mind. Sometimes I would thank Him for the breath that I took or the beautiful weather that day. I found that I didn't have to close my eyes (especially while driving) and I didn't even have to let on to the people around me what I was doing. God can read your thoughts and hear your heart. By doing this, I would take the opportunity to talk to my Savior and Creator at least fifteen times a day. Over time this trained me to spend my day in prayer without the use of a watch alarm. Now I begin my day with a few minutes of prayer, and then I spend moments of time throughout the day in prayer. I treat my day as one long conversation with God that seems more like a chat than a prayer. As I go to sleep at night, I conclude the prayer by thanking God for the day and praying for tomorrow. I truly believe that what Paul meant in 1 Thessalonians 5:17 was to have the ambiance of prayer in your daily life. I believe that this verse suggests a consciousness and awareness of God throughout your day.

I would be willing to bet that if you tried this for just one week, you would discover two things.

First of all, you would find that you have become a kinder, more Christlike person because you have set your mind on heavenly things by spending part of every hour in prayer. Also, you would feel the closeness of God in your life. As you speak to Him, He will seem nearer, and you will find that you are more tuned in to hear Him speaking back to you. I have been practicing this discipline of continuous prayer for over ten years, and I can tell you that I am far more in tune to what God is saying to me now than I was a decade ago.

PRIVATE WORSHIP

Worship is praise to God. It is very important as you grow in your faith and should be our number one focus as Christians. Worship is the fulfillment of what Jesus said is our most important responsibility which is to love Him with all our hearts, souls, minds, and strength.[100] When most Christians think about worship, they think about singing at church or a weekly worship service. Worship is not an event; it is a lifestyle. An interesting approach to understanding music's role in worship comes from a book titled *Worship—A Way of Life*[101] by Patrick Kavanaugh. In the book, Kavanaugh tells a story of a neighbor who you barely know, but who wants to get to know you better. So the neighbor finds a mutual friend and has that friend set up a dinner so the three of you can hang out. At dinner, you get to know each other and find that you have a lot in common. Soon you become friends with the neighbor. When the moral of this story is revealed, you learn that the neighbor represents God, and your friend who brought the two of you together symbolizes the role of music in worship. Music is the "introducer" between you and God in the setting of worship. Opportunities for group worship (also called corporate worship) are very important, providing an opportunity to express yourself to God with friends and fellow believers in Christ.

As significant to your faith as corporate worship can be, focusing on developing a pattern for private, personal worship will help you mature and know God more deeply. Worship, like prayer, does not have to be done in a large group setting with the help of a band or a pastor. Worship is anything you do to praise God. Private worship is being alone with God. In Psalm 46:10 God says to "Be still, and know that I am God."[102] Matthew 6:6 says, "When you pray, go away by yourself, shut the door behind you, and pray to your Father secretly."[103]

Over the past few years, I have discovered the joy of solitude. To me, solitude is an extended time away to be alone with God. I will be the first to admit that in the busy world that we live in, this is a very hard thing to do. The reason I started having a time of solitude was because when I was on staff with Young Life, they "required" it for all staff. I put quotes around the word "required" because it seems silly to require someone to take time to spend with God, but that is often what it takes. Over the years I have grown so much because of these times of solitude. Thomas Merton, a monk from the mid-twentieth century, wrote, "For the first time in my life I am finding you, O Solitude ...The speech of God is silence. His Word is solitude. Him I will never deny, by His grace!"104

My time of solitude is usually a once-a-month time that complements my daily morning quiet time. I'm sure that you don't struggle with this, but for me, my daily time in the Word is often unfocused and many times rushed because of my schedule. Because of this, I am grateful for these planned times of solitude. During my times of solitude, depending on how much time I have given myself, I take along a few things that fit my own personal worship style. For example, I love music. I am a music fan and a musician at heart. I love music as a part of worship and always bring my iPod, second only to my Bible. Also, I take my prayer journal and possibly a devotional book that I might be into at that time. (Strangely enough, Skittles have found their way into my personal worship style as well. I'm not sure how that happened, but it is true!) If I have a few hours, I go to a certain park and sit under a tree by a pond. If I have a whole day reserved, I find a more comfortable place such as a lake house or an empty room at my church. Either way, I turn the cell phone off, get offline, and focus on Christ. During this time of solitude, I find peace and rest for my soul.

MY PERSONAL WORSHIP STYLE

On my iPod I have thousands of songs. Depending on my mood, I pick something to get me focused on Christ. It helps me focus and sets the mood for worship. There are literally thousands of good worshipful songs that might appeal to you. Sometimes I choose a more traditional set of hymns, classical music, or even some "nonreligious" music that I find very worshipful.

Then, I usually spend time praying—nothing specific, but rather just whatever is on my heart and mind at the time. Sometimes prayer will dominate the majority of the time I have, and other times it will only focus me deeper in worship.

The next thing I like to do is read. Most of the time it is a section of the Scriptures or possibly a devotional or spiritual growth book. Over the years I have read devotional books like *My Utmost for His Highest* or books of meditation from Thomas Merton and Saint Francis. I have also been challenged by books by more modern authors that I like. Most often, during this time of solitude I will read a selection of Scripture that I have been studying or something that comes to mind while praying.

The last thing I do is write in my prayer journal. My journal is a collection of thoughts, prayers, ideas, dreams, and personal writings. I often go back to reread those prayers and either update my thoughts on the situation or look to see how God answered that prayer. I also like to make a list of people I need to pray for.

After I go through this semi-routine, and if I am planning to spend more time in solitude, I will go back to the iPod and put on more music, be still, and listen, as I get rest for my soul. This is often the only time that I am mentally turned off to the world.

I challenge you to discover your own personal worship style so that you will be comfortable when you sit down to pray and worship God. Chances are your style won't look exactly like mine. I have many friends who aren't into music or writing like I am. Some people find peace in praying and fasting all day (as I've just confessed, fasting is not as common in my solitude as it probably should be). You have to look at your own heart and let that dictate how you spend time alone with God. The most important thing is that you do spend time away. Pick a surrounding that won't be distracting (not in front of the TV or in bed) but will be comfortable and worshipful (outside under a tree, in a park by a lake, at a desk in the school library, on a couch with a blanket ...). Give yourself time to wind down and forget about all you have to do later that day. Turn on some music and begin to focus your thoughts on God. Think about how thankful you are, and then get lost in His presence. If I were a doctor, I would write you a prescription for this to be taken often.

GROWTH THROUGH JOURNALING

A journal has been a key component to my growth as a Christian over the past decade, and I believe that most people will find the same is true for them. A journal serves as a visual reminder of your thoughts, prayers, and struggles. As you write, your mind is focused in reflection on your life and walk with Christ. It also serves as an expression to God as you write your prayers to Him. For me, it forces me to think about what I want to pray about. Before I began journaling, my prayer time consisted of me sitting down to pray and then spending ten minutes of unconscious daydreaming before realizing what was happening. Now I have a blank page in a book that I want to fill. I have to think about what is going on in my life and focus myself on God. If you have never had a prayer journal, grab an old notebook, turn off the TV, and start writing whatever comes to mind. Think about what you want to say to God and begin to worship Him on paper. A prayer journal is a great place to write out a list of things that you want to continue praying about. Have you ever felt guilty because someone sincerely asked you to pray for them, and you committed to do it but then forgot? Write it in your prayer journal. These days you can keep that list more handy through technology. I have an app on my cell phone and computer that are linked together. If I hear a prayer request that I need to remember, I can list it immediately and then have it to pray for later. Prayer is such a cornerstone of our growth that we need to do whatever we can to keep it active.

A NEW KIND OF FREEDOM

Life is a journey. It's an adventure that can be exciting and full of joy and purpose. But, as you get older, you are finding out that life is also about choices. Good or bad, the daily choices you make now will affect the rest of your life. With choices comes freedom. Freedom to do anything you want to do. The older you get, the more freedom you will have, and the more impacting your decisions will be. That is why now is the time to make that most important decision to take your faith to the next level by learning to own it.

We have now spent eight chapters discussing how to do it. You must learn to focus your mind on Christ, but remember, this is not an overnight result. That's why it is called a journey. Take it one day at a time, each moment growing closer through prayer, reading the Bible, surrounding yourself with other believers, and making good, wise decisions.

Being a Christian in college can be an awesome experience. You have more opportunities to grow in your faith now than in years past. Yes, college is about freedom, but the journey with Christ is a new kind of freedom!

MY PRAYER FOR YOU

Abba Father—You are so awesome! Your blessings are far beyond what the mind can comprehend. I thank You for my friends reading this book—for their hearts, their passion for life, and their desire to know You. You are truly the way, life, and truth, and I pray as my friends continue on this journey that You will reveal yourself to them every day of their lives. Be with them in their struggles and their victories; be in their hard days and their great days. Celebrate with them as they succeed in life, and carry them when they fall. I pray that they will transform their minds to You, experience life to the full, and live their lives worthy of the calling You have given them. Jesus, I join them in praise for You. It's in Your peace that I pray. Amen.

ADDITIONAL RESOURCES
SECTION FOUR

Study Guide
FOR LOST IN TRANSITION

Chapter One
BOUND TO CHANGE

The main point of this chapter was:

Memory Verse:
Romans 6:23

From page 18 of the book, make a list below of a few things that you would like to change or develop about yourself before beginning college.

How do you typically handle change?

Who/What have been the biggest influences that have caused you the most growth in your faith thus far in your life? Describe how these influences helped you grow.

What are the things that have caused you to drift away from God and have kept you from growing stronger in your faith?

How do you think you will handle similar types of obstacles in college? Do you think it will be easier or harder to manage your faith in college?

NOTES:

Chapter Two
WHO DO YOU THINK YOU ARE?

The main point of this chapter was:

Memory Verse:
John10:10

How do other people usually describe me?
Why is it important to know who you are before
going off to college?

How is the concept of Spiritual Identity Theft
personified in the life of the average
college student?

If you were to ask 10 friends (some from school, some from church, etc.) to describe you, what would they say about the kind of person you are? What would they say about your faith, your witness, and your friendship?

What are the weaknesses in your life that the thief could easily use to "kill, steal, and destroy" your identity in Christ?

In 1 Samuel 7 the Israelites placed a stone called an Ebenezer to remember how the Lord had helped them. What can be an Ebenezer in your life to remind you how God has guided and helped you?

NOTES:

Chapter Three
COLLEGE LIFE

The main point of this chapter was:

Memory Verse:
James 4:7

Look back at the differences you listed between high school and college. Which ones are the most extreme and what can you do to thrive in that new normal?

What is the typical tendency of someone experiencing freedom for the first time?

Think about your expectations of college. What are you excited about, and what are your fears about college?

Do you think that the typical stereotypes of college are true or possibly exaggerated? Explain your answer.

How can you prepare yourself for some of the social and spiritual challenges you will face while in college?

NOTES:

Chapter Four
OWN YOUR OWN

The main point of this chapter was:

Memory Verse:
Romans 12:2

What does the phrase "Faith Ownership" mean to you?

What does it mean to conform?

What does it mean to transform?

Why do you think so many Christian college freshman do not naturally continue growing in their faith from where they left off in high school?

Thinking back on your "ancient paths" (from Jeremiah 6:16), what are some of the spiritual lessons you have learned that might help you make wise decisions in college?

How can you begin transforming your mind for Christ while in college? List ways in which you think you could make Romans 12:2 real in your life.

NOTES:

Chapter Five
WORDS OF WISDOM

The main point of this chapter was:

Memory Verse:
James 1:5

How do you typically make decisions, large or small? What are they based on, and how much time do you take to process the decision?

Do you consider yourself good at making decisions? Why or why not?

What is discipline, and why is it the key to developing wisdom? In what ways do you use discipline in your life right now?

Who do you consider a wise person? What wisdom have they given to you in the past, and what did you do with that wisdom?

Think back to a bad decision that you have made in the past year. How could you have used the Wisdom Filter in that situation to bring about a better result?

NOTES:

Chapter Six
THE WITNESS PROTECTION PROGRAM

The main point of this chapter was:

Memory Verse:
Matthew 5:14-16

What is an ambassador, and what does it mean to
be an ambassador for Christ?

Why is finding a church and plugging into a
Christian community important to your
spiritual growth in college?

What advice does the book offer in the following four categories? Think of at least one major point for each topic.

Joining a Greek Organization

Dating

Dealing with Professors

Drinking Alcohol

How do you agree or disagree with these statements?

How do you plan to balance being a social
Christian in college at parties, with dates, and
dealing with the pressures that will come because
of your faith?

NOTES:

Chapter Seven
GIVING YOUR LIFE AWAY

The main point of this chapter was:

Memory Verse:
Ephesians 4:1

What gifts, passions, and hobbies do you have that God might use to further His Kingdom?

According to the book, what does it mean to be in full-time ministry?

What does it mean to live your life worthy of the calling you have received?

What is a mission statement, and how could a personal mission statement change the way you live and make decisions?

Developing your own personal mission statement. This is not something that you should do quickly, off the top of your head. Rather, this statement should be something that you think and pray about as you construct a statement that will define how you see yourself and your life in Christ. Write this statement below and then copy it somewhere where you will see it often.

NOTES:

Chapter Eight
SET APART

The main point of this chapter was:

Memory Verse:
Ephesians 1:4

According to the chapter, what does it mean to "think like God"? What are some examples where thinking spiritually can apply to your life?

What does it mean to pray continually?

What is the difference in public and private worship?

Write out a description of your personal worship style. Are you driven by music? Does keeping a journal interest you? When is a good time to schedule a time of private worship within the next week? Make a plan and try to stick to it.

Write a prayer to God. In this prayer, tell Him how you are doing. Write out what you have learned in this book and what you plan to do to own your own faith. In this prayer, ask Him to help you weather the storms of college and life and to remain faithful to Him during your most tempting moments. After writing this prayer, come back to it often and let it serve as a visual reminder of your commitment to Jesus.

TRANSITION YEAR MATERIALS

ADDED RESOURCES FOR YOUR TRANSITION YEAR, WHICH IS THE CALENDAR YEAR OF YOUR GRADUATION
(LAST SEMESTER OF HIGH SCHOOL AND FIRST SEMESTER OF COLLEGE).

Content index:

A New Year's Challenge For Seniors
(best read in January of senior year)

What does New Year's mean to you? ...fun with friends, watching a big ball dramatically drop in Times Square, or maybe it's just another number added on the calendar? Regardless of what you think about it, New Year's is about change. But not only change from one year to the next, it represents a new beginning. Every year the whole word resets itself. Financially, one fiscal year ends and another begins. In nature, leaves and flowers die in the fall and begin to bloom again in the early months of the new year. Even our culture revolves around a calendar that stops and starts again in January. New Year's is about re-starting; it's about everything being new again.

There is no doubt that this is a year that you have been awaiting for a long time. At some point, in early elementary school days, someone did the math and said that you would be in the class of 20??. I'm sure that hearing that date back then would have seemed so far in the future that it would have been hard to comprehend. But now that has all changed. For you this whole year will represent change. Soon you will begin your last semester of high school, and later this year you will start your first semester of college...talk about new beginnings.

There is no better time than now to get on the right track and begin to prepare for this exciting year. More than starting a new year, when I think about new beginnings, I think about Jesus. In Revelation 21:5 Jesus says, "I am making everything new." In 2 Corinthians 5:17, Paul writes,

"Therefore, if anyone is in Christ, the new creation has come: The old has gone, the new is here!" Jesus offers us, not only life, but a newness to life that is recurring and refreshing.

I want to challenge you to think in these terms this week: How can you let God renew in your life that will prepare you for this year? You know that when you go off to college this fall you will meet and become friends with a lot of new people. What type of person do you want to be when you meet those new friends? Now is the time to ask these questions and let God mold you into the person He created you to be.

GOING DEEPER

Write out a description of the person you want to be the day you start college. Consider all aspects of your life: physically, emotionally, academically, socially, and spiritually. Be honest and realistic. Remember, you should be focused on the person God created you to be and not the person that will make you more popular on campus. This means you need to pray throughout this whole process. What do you think it will take to become more like this person? For example, if you want to be more organized or more disciplined with time management, then you need to think about writing down your schedule, putting things on a calendar, etc. If you want to be more knowledgeable in scripture, then set yourself up to learn a verse per week, etc. As with anything this year, feel free to ask me for help. This week read 2 Corinthians 5. This is a great chapter about new beginnings.

Planning For A Great Year
(best read in January or February of senior year)

If you recently celebrated New Year's Day, then I am sure that you still can't believe that it is the year of your graduation! It always takes me the first 6 months of each year to remember not to write last year's date. I don't know about you, but I like starting a new year. I like to start over with a clean slate. To me, a new year means new goals and experiences, and a chance to make this year the best yet.

For you, this year is not just any year, it is a graduation year and the beginning of your Transition Year to college. For all of us, the new year can be one of great accomplishment with many unknown possibilities. This year, for the most part, will be what you want it to be. Sure, there will be many things that will happen this year that will be out of our control, but how we react and deal with those things will be what truly makes the difference.

Many people make New Year's resolutions: personal commitments of self improvement like losing weight, exercising more, or playing more Playstation (well, maybe not that one). I think New Year's resolutions are great, in theory; it is important to have personal goals and a proper perspective of life for the year to come. One thing I've noticed is that most resolutions are about outward, physical changes, but what about making a commitment to grow in your faith? I truly believe that if we can focus on our relationship with Jesus and make our walk with Christ a priority, then this will be the best year ever. I also know that this is easier said than done. Like many New Year's resolutions, we commit to strengthen our faith in the coming year, and may do great for a few days or weeks; but then we get distracted and sidetracked and find ourselves back in the same place on New Year's Day the next year.

So, what do you think about making this year an exception to that rule? Why not make this year of great year of growth in Christ? I know you can do it...that is if you really want to. Here's what we will do. Below is an exercise in spiritual goal setting. Follow each instruction and you will be on your way to living closer to those goals this year. Then, there will continue to be content on this blog, throughout the year, to remind and help you with your progress. Here are 6 things to do to begin:

- Take out a piece of paper or find a blank sheet in a notebook or journal.
- Ask and answer this question to yourself: *What was my walk with Christ like last year?*
- Ask and answer this question to yourself: *What were the moments of growth and struggle last year?*
- Ask and answer this question to yourself: *If I could do anything this year to mature in my faith, what would I do?*
- Share your answers with a friend who will keep you accountable for them.
- Keep this list close to you and review and pray over it often.

Five Questions For Thinking Correctly About Your Transition To College
(best read in the spring of senior year)

In a few short months from now, you will begin living as a college student in an new environment and setting. The goal for you, between now and then, is to continue to get prepared. Romans 12:2 says that in order to live a life transformed, you must begin to renew your mind. This means that before you can make a healthy transition to college, you must first think correctly about your transition to college. Here are five questions that you can ask yourself to continue thinking correctly about that transition:

1. What are the key components to my spiritual growth, right now in high school, and how will I continue that growth in college?

2. How well do I manage my time and what do I need to work on before I begin college?

3. What are my study habits in high school, and how do I plan to make good grades in college?

4. Am I dependent or independent when it comes to being around friends/peers all the time?

5. How well do I make decisions on a daily basis and where do my decisions usually lead me?

Great Expectations: 4 Goals For College
(best read in the spring of senior year)

When my wife and I were engaged, we were challenged to come up with our expectations for marriage. We had no idea what married life would be like but we were excited to experience it together. We developed expectations and then formed some goals to reach those expected desires.

Anytime you face a life transition, it is very important to have goals and expectations. Even though, on the surface, goal setting doesn't sound like a fun thing to do, it might be a way to insure yourself the college experience that you've always hoped for (and that does sound like fun). Below are four goals that I hope you will have in college:

1. **Lasting Memories.** Everyone wants to go to college and make lasting memories. In part, college is made for moments like that. There is not a college student on earth that doesn't want to make lasting memories during this new, exciting chapter of life. Those years in college will be some of the best years of your life. You will have more time, more freedom, (maybe) more funds, and probably more friends. The main question to ask yourself is how will you handle those moments.

2. **Deep Relationships.** College is a very social time and you will make many friends in the process. But, I hope that you won't just make good friendships, rather I hope that you will make deep relationships. This means that you will live life together, sharing experiences and being real with

them. The main question to ask yourself is what will your relationships be based on?

Let's stop here for a moment. There is no doubt that all college students would like to have lasting memories and deep relationships as two goals for college. This is no huge discovery with these first two goals, and if we stopped here, you would enter college like the majority of college freshmen. Here are the final two goals that will set you apart from the average Joe Freshman.

3. **Clear Vision.** Everyone has dreams and hopes in life, but very few actually ever have a clear vision of the path in front of them. A clear vision includes developing wisdom, gaining insight, and understanding what God has called them to. Having clarity in your future pursues will help you feel more confident and purposeful in your life as you graduate and move into the "real world." The main question to ask yourself is will you be able to see it?

4. **Fruitful Faith.** Notice, I didn't simply say a "strong faith" or just a "relationship with Jesus." If you are a follower of Christ, I hope you do have a growing, strong relationship with Jesus, but as a college goal, I hope that your faith in Christ will be fruitful; meaning, that it produces. Think of an Apple Tree. It is worthless if it does not produce apples. This is a sign of someone who understands the meaning of what Jesus teaches in Matthew 5 about being the Light of the World and the Salt of the Earth. The main question to ask yourself is will you be ready when God gives you the chance to change lives?

So, now that I have given you four goals to have in college, let me ask two questions. First, what order do you prioritize them in? Secondly, how do you reach these goals? The answer to both questions is found in the same answer. Even though I gave you the goals in this order: Lasting Memories, Deep Relationships, Clear Vision, & Fruitful Faith, the truth is they are in opposite order of priority. A fruitful faith is the foundation. If you place any other of the three as a foundation, it will be shaky ground. A clear vision is your direction, lead by your fruitful faith. The deep relationships are the substance of your time in college, and the lasting memories are the result of the other three. Now, with that said, how do you reach these goals? Focus on developing a fruitful faith, and all the others will fall into place. If you stand firm on the foundation of your faith, it will be fruitful, it will give you clear vision for your future, you will have deep relationships, and lasting memories.

GOING DEEPER
1. What are your expectations of college? What do you hope to get out of this chapter of life?
2. How important is it to you to make goals and do whatever it takes to stick to them?
3. Why do you think most college students do not make goals or set expectations for themselves in college?

Taking The 25:40 Challenge
(best read in the summer of transition year)

Truly I tell you, whatever you did for one of the least of these brothers and sisters of mine, you did for me. Matthew 25:40

This summer, before you transition to college, I want to challenge you to make a difference in the lives of others (and in yourself). The 25:40 Challenge, based on Matthew 25:40, is a way for you and your friends to do something out of the ordinary to give to the least of these. Here are 5 steps to plan for the challenge this summer:

1 Make the decision that you will take the challenge.

2 Think about what you would like to do. You could spend a couple Saturdays at a local homeless shelter or get some friends from school or church to take a short mission trip to some near or far off location (NOTE: if you already have a mission trip planned with your church, plan to do something outside of that pre-commitment).

3 Contact the person in charge and make arrangements to serve.

4 Make a list of things you hope God will show you during the experience.

5 Begin to pray about this commitment. Prepare to change lives, starting with your own.

Looking Back To See Ahead
(best read in the summer of transition year)

Here are ten questions for you to ask yourself to help you prepare for the transition to college. Spend time on these answers and allow them to challenge and sharpen you.

•When have you felt the strongest in your walk with Christ?

•When have you felt the weakest in your faith?

•What has caused the biggest spiritual growth spurts in the past 2 years?

•What are your biggest moral struggles, and what does it take for them to affect you?

•How has peer pressure affected you in the past year?

•What have you learned about yourself that could help you overcome (or cause you to fall to) peer pressure in college?

•How have Christian friends and mentors helped you grow in your faith this year and what have those relationships taught you about your need for community to grow in college?

•What mistake do you hope not to make in college?

•What are two or three qualities about yourself right now that you hope to change or mature while in college?

For those moving away to go to college:

•What are you going to miss most about not living at home with your family?

•What will you have to learn to do better before you live away from your family in college?

Preparing For Liftoff: 5 things to do before starting college.

(best read just before starting college)

Please buckle your seatbelt and prepare for liftoff. In just a matter of days/weeks, you will be launching into a new stratosphere of life. You are college bound. It won't be long now before you will be living the dorm life, taking that soon-to-be familiar walk to class, and meeting new friends that you will know for the rest of your life. Starting your freshman year in college is the beginning of an exciting new season of life. A lot is changing and even more change is just around the corner. To prepare for this journey, I want to give you five things that you should do before starting college.

1. Recruit A Prayer Team– Prayer is a necessity of a healthy spiritual life. This involves, not only praying often yourself, but also having other people regularly pray for you. Before you go off to college, find a team of people who will commit to pray for you daily. This shouldn't be hard to do. Any adult who has acted as a mentor in your life would gladly agree to such an offer. I suggest you ask 10 people to pray for you daily. You can even give them a list of specifics to pray for or you can email them once a month to update them on your prayer needs.

2. Talk Finances– Most likely, starting college will be the first time that you will be on your own financially. Even though the majority of college students still have their parents pay many of their bills, you will be responsible for your day to day

financial needs. Before classes start, sit down with your parents and talk about your financial situation. How will you be getting money to live on? Will you be required to get a job or will you get an allowance in college? How will you receive this money (direct deposit into a debit card account, credit card)? Also, it is important to make a budget for how you think you will spend this money. This is a great time in life to learn financial lessons before you get older and the stakes get higher.

3. List Your Non-Negotiables– A non-negotiable is something that, under no condition, will you ever do. In other words, it's a stand that you commit to make without negotiation. For example, I love my wife so much that I have made adultery a non-negotiable in my life. This means that, since I have vowed to never commit adultery, I must stay away from things that might tempt me in this way. You should already have an idea in your mind about what some non-negotiables in your life should be. It would be a very wise thing for you to make a list of these things before starting college. What are your non-negotiables regarding partying and drinking, dating and sexual temptation, health and wellness, friends and social groups, etc? Making these decisions before you are forced into those situations will be helpful as you work to be true to yourself and your relationship with Christ.

4. Learn The Practical Essentials– Living on your own is hard work. You have to be responsible for your time, money, possessions, and you have to know how to do things that you might not have had to do before. For example, when I moved off to college, I had to learn how to wash my own clothes.

I was not responsible for that at home and therefore had never done it before on my own. My wife, before going off to college, had never made a deposit at a bank, so she had to learn the process of filling out the deposit slip, knowing what to say to the teller, and making the deposit. It's okay if you are not yet familiar with doing these types of things, but now is the time to learn. Ask your parents or another adult about what normal, everyday responsibilities you might need to learn before going to college, and then learn how to do them.

5. Get Acclimated– Chances are you have already been to your college campus to visit &/or for orientation. You may or may not already know your roommate and have a room picked out. Chances are you have your class schedule, but you may not yet know how to get to your classes. Before you start college, it would be a good idea to get acclimated to college. For example, pull up a campus map and learn your way around. If you haven't already talked to your roommate, make the call. If you are unsure about what churches and campus ministries are available, go to the university web site and learn more about them. The more you know when you get to school, the more comfortable you will feel about starting to make the transition.

Finding A Church At College Before Thanksgiving
(best read just after starting college)

Finding a new church at college is a critical step in the process of connecting to new community. But, it is hard and, chances are, you have never had to do it before. So, here is a trick that you can use to find a new church, by Thanksgiving. Why Thanksgiving? Well, that way you can sit down for a big turkey dinner with your family and inform them, "I FOUND A CHURCH!!!" Here is the deal. Be sure you follow every step exactly like it is laid out.

First Week of College (or before): Find some friends who want to join in on the fun and find out which are the five best local churches in the area for you. You can ask older students, look online, or drive around and check out a few.

The First Sunday in September: Go to the first church on your list of five. Attend a worship event, find out what they have for college students, and talk to others who are there.

The Next Four Sundays: Do the same thing to the other four churches on your list of five.

The Second Sunday in October: Pick your top three churches and drop two from the list. Don't feel bad; this is important. Now, go back to those top three options for the next three weeks.
The Last Sunday in October: Pick your favorite two remaining churches and visit one of them. Be sure

Group Bundle Book Orders

Transition Bundle $15
(Lost in Transition & The Freedom Permit)

Ownership Bundle $15
(Ownership Road & Ownership RoadMap)

NAME _____

CHURCH _____

EMAIL _____

Bundle: Quantity: Price:

TRANSITION

OWNERSHIP

Total:

(Books will be delivered to you if not on site. Credit card
accepted now or check to me mailed within a week.)

to learn as much about this church as you can as it relates to your involvement.

The First Sunday in November: Go to the other church on your final list of two. After you do this, pick the one that you feel drawn to the most.

The Second Sunday in November: You have now picked a church. Go there and join. You have done a very thorough search for the right church and now you (and hopefully some friends) can jump in and become a valuable part of that community. Not to mention the whole, "guess what I did, mom/dad?" thing!

52 Challenging Transition Year Question

Below are 53 challenging question to help you keep a right perspective as you finish high school and begin college. You might want to find a friend to answer a question per week and keep each other accountable as you grow together.

Questions For High School Seniors (beginning in Jan):

- What do you hope to get out of your last semester of high school (other than a diploma)?
- What is your role/responsibility this year, in your school and church, as a high school senior?
- Who has been some of the biggest influence in your life and why?
- What are a few of the main lessons of faith that you have learned from these influences?
- What would you have to develop or change if you no longer had those influences in your life?
- In what ways did you look up to seniors when you were younger?
- What does it mean to be the Light of the World (see Matt 5:14)?
- Ephesians 4:1 says that we should "live our lives worthy of the calling we have received". What does that verse means to you in relation to how you see yourself at this stage of your life?
- How have you seen graduated seniors, older than you, go off to college and change from the way that they were in high school? How has that

affected the way you think about the transition to college?

- What have you learned in the past year about yourself and your faith that can carry you into a healthy spiritual transition into college?
- What struggles have you had this year and how will they affect you in college if you continue to have them?
- In what ways are you ready for college and in what ways are you not yet ready?
- How can you prepare now to grow in your walk with Christ in college?
- How do you want your relationship with Jesus to look one year from now?
- What are you most afraid of about going to college?
- What are you most excited about going to college?
- What does it mean to "finish well" in high school?
- What can you do this month to give back to those who have taught you and helped you grow as a person?
- What are your plans this summer to serve others?
- How will you spend your summer preparing for college?
- What are five things that you have learned about yourself in high school and how will recognizing those five things help you as you start college?

- What regrets do you have about high school and how will you either forget about them (because they are in the past) or let them challenge you to do better in the future?
- How does it feel to be a high school graduate? What responsibilities do you have in your family, with your friends, and in your community now?
- How grateful you are to your parents/family for their support of you in high school? Think about your answer, and let them know.
- What people do you want to spend time with this summer before you start college?
- What can you do this summer to spend quality time with your family?
- How is God challenging you this summer to mature and grow?
- How will you spend the rest of the summer preparing for college?
- How were you at time management, in high school, and what do you need to learn this summer to prepare to be more responsible in college?
- How were you at money management, in high school, and what do you need to learn this summer to prepare to be more responsible in college?

Questions For College Freshmen (beginning in Aug):

- What are your expectations for college (hope, dreams, goals)?
- What most excites you about starting college?
- What scares you the most about starting college?
- What are the characteristics of a good friend to have in college?
- What type of organizations do you want to be a part of on campus?
- What friends are you beginning to spend the most time with & do you share the same convictions?
- What are you doing socially that differs morally from your actions in high school?
- How are you growing in your faith now that you are in college?
- How would you define your emotional stability right now?
- Have the first few weeks of college been what you expected them to be? Why or why not?
- What qualities of leadership and serving do you have and how can you use them in your involvements in college?
- How have you grown in time management already in college? What do you still need to improve on?

- How have you grown in money management already in college? What do you still need to improve on?
- How would you compare your academic performance in college to that of high school?
- How would you compare your social life in college to that of high school?
- How would you compare your faith journey so far in college to that of high school?
- What are the things that are fueling you this fall? What gives you life?
- What are the things that are stealing life from you this fall?
- Now that mid-terms are over, how are you doing in your classes? What might you need to improve before finals?
- How can you make a mid-semester adjustment in your time management to fix some things?
- Are you fulfilling some of the goals that you made for your first semester in college?
- If you could evaluate your first semester in college, what grade would you give it academically, socially, emotionally, and spiritually?
- What will you have to do next semester to continue to grow and mature in your faith as you continue through your freshman year in college?

More About

THETRANSMISSION

TheTransMission is a ministry dedicated to helping high school seniors and college freshmen make a healthy, spiritual transition into college, founded by author/speaker Tommy McGregor. This mission is communicated through relationships between TheTransMission and local churches and ministries. Through online content, events, and curriculum, TheTransMission guides students through one of the most difficult spiritual transitions of their life.

TheTransMission website is an ongoing wealth of content throughout the year for students, parents, and ministry leaders as they walk through the Transition Year together. The site includes articles, videos, podcasts, devotionals, and more.

The senior events are opportunities for seniors to come together with fellow future graduates to be challenged with goals for college and a plan to reach those goals. These events can be in a one-night format or as a senior weekend retreat.

For more on the ministry, go to the website at www.thetransmission.org and follow on Facebook at www.facebook.com/TransMissionOrg.

More About
TOMMY MCGREGOR

Tommy McGregor is an author, speaker, ministry coach/consultant, and the founder of TheTransMission, a ministry devoted to guiding students through to a healthy spiritual transition of life after high school. He is the author of *Ownership Road: Leading Our Children To An Authentic Faith That Prepares Them For Life After High School*, *Lost in Transition: Becoming Spiritually Prepared for College*, *The Freedom Permit: Creating A Vision of Discipleship for your Senior's Last Year of High School*, and *Selfie: A Parent's Guide to Social Media*. Tommy has spent over two decades in ministry working with teenagers, parents, and ministry leaders, and is passionate about helping others develop a sense of who God has created them to be. He lives in Montgomery, AL with his wife and their two boys.

Tommy can be reached via email at tommy@tommymcgregor.com, as well as on Twitter at @tommymcgregor and Facebook at www.facebook.com/TommyMcGregorAuthor.

END NOTES

[1] Just kidding about that one.

[2] This statistic is an average of a few reliable stats. The range is about 70-85 percent.

[3] John 10:10b niv

[4] Captain Kangaroo was a great show for kids. I always liked Mister Greenjeans the best.

[5] 2 Corinthians 5:17 nlt

[6] Michael Jordan stats can be found at www.nba.com.

[7] Romans 3:23 niv

[8] Romans 6:23 niv

[9] John Stott, Basic Christianity (Inter-Varsity Press, 1958) page 130.

[10] Information about the Alamo can be found at www.drtl.org/History/index.asp

[11] www.Younglife.org/wilderness

[12] Luke 5:6-11 nlt

[13] The Chronicles of Narnia

[14] The Lord of the Rings

[15] Harry Potter

[16] Toy Story

[17] Genesis 3:1-7 niv

[18] wikipedia/alfrednobel

[19] Braveheart, Mel Gibson (Paramount Pictures, Icon Productions/Ladd Company, 1995).

[20] 1 Corinthians 3:2 nlt

[21] Read James 4:7

[22] Ephesians 5:18 nlt

[23] niv

[24] Quote taken from www.smu.edu/alec/ whyhighschool.html

[25] http://www.motortrend.com/

[26] Josh McDowell Ministry can be found at www.josh.org

[27] "With more than 15 million copies in print, More Than a Carpenter continues to be one of the most powerful evangelism tools worldwide. In a concise, understandable manner, Josh explains how Jesus' life and the testimony of history unmistakably affirm his claim to be God." (Josh.org)

[28] Jeremiah 6:16 niv

[29] Romans 12:2 niv

[30] NLT

[31] Survivor first aired on May 31, 2000 on CBS.

[32] The Voice first premiered on April 26, 2011 on NBC. The coaches consisted of Christina Aguilera, Cee Lo Green, Adam Levine, and Blake Shelton.

[33] Putting on the Hits first aired on September 15, 1984, on CBS.

[34] Transformers, Michael Bay (Dreamworks Pictures, May 3, 2007).

[35] Transformers Action Figures from Hasbro— www.transformers.com

[36] NLT

[37] Galatians 5:1 NIV

[38] Luke 15:11-24 niv

[39] Brian Vander Ark, "The Freshman" (RCA Music Group, 1996).

[40] John 14:16-17

[41] Ephesians 5:15-17 NASB

[42] Mark Matlock, Freshman: The College Student's Guide to Developing Wisdom (NavPress, 2005).

[43] Proverbs 3:13-18 NLT

[44] 1 Samuel 13:14, Acts 13:22

[45] 1 Kings 3:5, 9-12 nlt

[46] NLT

[47] Andy Stanley, The Best Question Ever (Multnomah, 2004).

[48] Andy Stanley, The Best Question Ever, Page 28

[49] Andy Stanley, The Best Question Ever, Page 12

50 Mark Matlock, Freshman: The College Student's Guide to Developing Wisdom, Page 37

51 1 Kings 3:23-27 niv

52 Ephesians 4:21-24 nlt

53 www.usmarshals.gov

54 Dave Roberts, Following Jesus: A Non-Religious Guidebook for the Spiritually Hungry (Relevant Books, 2004).

55 NLT

56 NLT

57 www.sharptopcove.yl.org

58 The Message

59 NLT

60 NIV

61 Matthew 6:16-18

62 USA Today poll by Joseph Popiolkowshi and Adrienne Lewis. Source: Higher Education Research Institute at UCLA.

63 www.cru.org

64 www.YoungLife.org

65 www.campusoutreach.org

66 www.fca.org

67 NLT

[68] The Toughest Test in College: Why Students are Failing to Keep Their Faith on Campus DVD (Focus on the Family, 2009).

[69] Josh McDowell, Don't Check Your Brains at the Door (W Publishing Group, 1992) p. 112-113.

[70] NIV

[71] NLT

[72] NLT

[73] NIV

[74] NLT

[75] Seeing U2's "With or Without You" video was a major moment in my teenage years (for obvious reasons).

[76] 1 Corinthians 12:4-5

[77] Philippians 1:6

[78] NLT

[79] Chick-fil-A is the best of the best in all things food—www.chick-fil-a.com

[80] Krispy Kreme will be served in heaven—www.krispykreme.com

[81] NLT

[82] NLT

[83] NLT

[84] Romans 12:1-2 NIV

85 NLT

86 The Message

87 NLT

88 NLT

89 NLT

90 The Mahabharata 5:1517

91 The Talmud, Shabbat 31a

92 Udana-Varga 5:18

93 Number 13 of Imam, "Al-Nawawi's Forty Hadiths"

94 NLT

95 Mark 12:30, Luke 10:27

96 NLT

97 NLT

98 NLT

99 NIV

100 Mark 12:30, Luke 10:27

101 Patrick Kavanaugh, Worship—A Way Of Life (Chosen Books, 2001).

102 NIV

103 NLT

[104] Thomas Merton, A Year with Thomas Merton: Daily Meditations from His Journals, (Harper: San Francisco, 2004) page 4.

74231530R00141

Made in the USA
Columbia, SC
30 July 2017